unwind
your
mind

unwind your mind

The life-changing power of ASMR

Emma WhispersRed

RIDER
LONDON • SYDNEY • AUCKLAND • JOHANNESBURG

1 3 5 7 9 10 8 6 4 2

Rider, an imprint of Ebury Publishing,
20 Vauxhall Bridge Road,
London SW1V 2SA

Rider is part of the Penguin Random House group of companies
whose addresses can be found at global.penguinrandomhouse.com

Penguin
Random House
UK

First published in Great Britain by Rider in 2019

www.penguin.co.uk

A CIP catalogue record for this book is available from the
British Library

ISBN 9781846046230

Typeset in 11.5/17 pt Sabon LT Std
by Integra Software Services Pvt. Ltd, Pondicherry

Printed and bound in Great Britain by Clays Ltd, Elcograf S.p.A.

MIX
Paper from
responsible sources
FSC
www.fsc.org FSC® C018179

Penguin Random House is committed to a sustainable
future for our business, our readers and our planet.
This book is made from Forest Stewardship Council®
certified paper.

To my family

Contents

Preface

My memory is of a beautiful summer day in our little English village. My friend and I are at the local swing park, chatting away as we go up and down on the seesaw, bikes lying on the ground beside us. We can't have been more than ten years old. 'Do you get that thing where you're not really here, but you are? And a sort of crinkly and fuzzy feeling in your head?' I ask. It is the first time I mention my special thing to anyone else.

I see a confused look appear on her face, 'I think so ... Maybe ... Er ... No, not really, I don't think.' The subject quickly changes to something way more interesting, like who got to sneak a look at the *Just Seventeen* problem pages or how many penny sweets we can buy ourselves today. I still remember that moment vividly.

Growing up as a sensitive and quiet child was for me, let's say, quite tricky. When your inner world is rich but your confidence to be outwardly expressive is poor, many things are difficult to explain. Maybe my friend did experience what I was asking about, but how do you talk about a feeling that doesn't have a name? Thankfully now we do have a name for the glorious feeling I was trying to describe as a child, and now I – and the millions of people who share this experience with me – are more able to express it. It's called ASMR – Autonomous Sensory Meridian Response – and in this book I will explain what it is and how you can experience and benefit from it yourself.

My name is Emma Smith. I work full time as an ASMRtist creating content for my three YouTube channels: WhispersRed ASMR, WhispersRed Sleepy Children and My Purple Life. I have been an ASMRtist for the last six years and I film my videos in a mostly soundproof studio at the end of my garden. It's called 'The Tingle Shed'. I am also a qualified sound healing practitioner with the College of Sound Healing in England and reiki practitioner with the Reiki Academy London, which all came about after my discovery of ASMR.

Over the years I seem to have become a sort of 'Internet Mother' to many, which I lovingly and gratefully accept. It's very much an honour as this special ASMR 'feeling' really has become a life mission for me and, you could say, my child. I'm a very protective 'mum' and we've been through a lot together. I never felt like a 'YouTuber' in the way I assume most people think of it. The culture of 'likes', 'subscribers', 'tags' and views often feels a little odd, though I am very grateful for the platform as a way to reach and connect with so many like-minded people. I feel that the internet should be used wherever possible as a tool for positive connection and for bringing people together, so I work a lot outside of my YouTube channels and see them as a way to build a community, a base from which to explore other possibilities and expand awareness of ASMR in other realms of society.

In 2015 I organised and hosted the first live ASMR event and have since established live ASMR as an accepted concept in several different formats in London, Berlin, San Francisco and New York – from ASMR sessions in a theatre with wireless headsets to an immersive 'ASMR Spa', and even an interactive ASMR exhibition in conjunction with a brand.

I am happy to talk about and represent ASMR as much as I can with the press, so have spoken with many news outlets around the world, and by the time you read this I will hopefully be on my way to releasing an ASMR music album. I'm also presenting an ASMR podcast for the first time, which is a lot of fun. It is really great to get out there and bring awareness of ASMR to groups of people who may not have come across it otherwise. I like to have the chance to explain it in a way that can be understood and hopefully help someone who may need it.

I aim to support ASMR as a legitimate therapeutic experience for all living beings (yes, animals experience it too) and will continue these activities for as long as I can.

My absolute dream is for ASMR to become a recognised complementary therapy available to all, to teach people everywhere and to open an ASMR retreat centre. If you can, please cross all your fingers and toes on my behalf; I'd be very grateful. I am crossing all of mine for you to manifest your dreams too.

Now feels like the right time to write a book about this topic and to discuss it on a heart-led level. I do this very humbly with the hope that I can positively support and represent ASMR with all its complexities, not only for the existing community around the world but also for those discovering it for the first time. Perhaps you know what I was trying to explain to my friend when I was little? You may have had similar conversations growing up. Maybe you have already heard about ASMR through a friend, in a news article or hopping around YouTube? Hopefully you're in for a treat and are about to discover a whole new world.

In *Unwind your Mind: The Life-Changing Power of ASMR,* I explain what ASMR is from my own experiences, its history and how it arrived into popular culture. How you can learn to embrace this sensation to ease stress and anxiety, to improve sleep and how to explore its simple calming effects to support physical and mental wellbeing. Through practical information, tips and simple guided exercises, I will guide you to find your own personal ASMR sensitivity and understand how we can use it to promote self-awareness and self-development.

You will also hear my personal story of how I found the ASMR community, how ASMR became a therapy for me, how it completely changed my life and how it changed the way I live and love now. It's been a journey for sure.

The videos I make are with the intention to create a calm and quiet haven for the viewer and a sanctuary. It isn't always the right place for me to discuss the full range of subjects I am interested in surrounding ASMR, my personal thoughts, theories about it and things I have learned so far in depth. My channel is an intuitive place and I try to keep it free of too much thinking. For this reason I am grateful for an opportunity to write at length about a subject that has been close to me my whole life and that I have studied every day for the last six years.

I would also like this book to serve as some assistance for current new ASMRtists and those wishing to take the leap to become one. Either as a step towards their own healing, for that of others or both. To perhaps give them some inspiration from my experiences and thoughts on what our purpose is as facilitators for healing.

The wonderful thing about ASMR is that it's totally universal; it transcends everything and brings people together. I am aware that I speak to people of all ages, location, experience, knowledge and background. Some of this information will be preaching to the converted so to speak, to some it will be completely new. I hope there is something in here for everyone.

Foreword

For as long as I can remember I've experienced a warm tingling sensation that starts in the top of my head, spreads like a wave down my spine and lulls me into an almost trance-like state of relaxation. This feeling would emerge at different moments during childhood: when I was getting my feet measured for school shoes, having a teacher explain things carefully, watching my mum brush her hair, and during soft-spoken conversations with friends during sleepovers. I'd always assumed that this feeling was an unusual personal quirk. I'd asked my sister if she felt the same thing. She didn't and so I kept it to myself. Then, in 2013, I discovered I wasn't the only one.

I'm a psychologist and I was at a conference. After listening to a softly spoken talk (I can't even remember what the topic was!), I told a colleague that the speaker's voice made me feel tingly and relaxed. She said that what I described sounded similar to something she'd seen in the media about a fascination with towel-folding tutorials. When I got home, I immediately searched online.

I soon discovered the wonderful world of ASMR and the online community. After I'd spent a few hours watching ASMR videos, I started hunting for research on the topic. Surely if this feeling had a name and was something that others also experienced then there must be research on it?

All I could find was one sentence in an article describing a case study of an individual with a specific type of synaesthesia (a crossing of the senses where she would taste words). As far as I could tell there hadn't been any research studies on ASMR. This is an immensely unique situation because even unusual and very rare experiences typically have some literature behind them. I began talking to colleagues and friends about ASMR: did they experience it too and why had no one done any research on it? I realised that there was a heavy dose of scepticism among people who didn't experience ASMR – the feeling wasn't familiar and showing YouTube videos often resulted in disbelief – 'You're telling me that you find this *relaxing*?!' – and sometimes judgement.

What would it take to convince those who do not experience ASMR that it is a genuine experience? Along with my colleagues, Drs Emma Blakey, Tom Hostler and Theresa Veltri, I conducted a series of studies in 2014, which were published in our 2018 paper: 'More than a Feeling: Autonomous Sensory Meridian Response (ASMR) is characterised by reliable changes in affect and physiology', which you can read freely online.[1] We wanted to scientifically test the idea that ASMR is a relaxing experience rather than relying on anecdotal reports. To design our studies, we took inspiration from the better-researched phenomenon of music-induced chills (the shivers down the spine and goosebumps that some people experience in response to music). Our research consistently shows that for ASMR-sensitive individuals the state of ASMR increases feelings of relaxation, calm and social connectedness. Importantly, we discovered that ASMR videos significantly lowers the heart rate in all those viewing it, and in ASMR-sensitive individuals more so than those who are not ASMR-sensitive. Our studies now provide scientific evidence in support of the idea that ASMR is relaxing – it isn't just people telling us that ASMR makes them feel relaxed, their physiology is telling us the same thing too.

What's notable is that the reductions in heart rate we observed in ASMR-sensitive individuals were comparable to stress reduction techniques such as mindfulness and listening to music. Anecdotally, people who experience ASMR use videos to help with stress, insomnia, depression, anxiety and loneliness. Although we don't have the data to back up their effectiveness for clinical conditions, our research does provide preliminary

---

[1] bit.ly/2IngdyP

evidence that ASMR imparts physiological and emotional benefits to experiencers.

Our group is not the only one to research ASMR. I've been thrilled to see increasing numbers of ASMR research papers following the first ASMR study published by Emma Barratt and Nick Davis in 2015. A small but growing body of studies has started to: characterise and measure the ASMR experience (Natalie Roberts and colleagues), describe how and what people use it for (Barratt and Davis), catalogue common triggers and highlight patterns of brain activation when individuals experience ASMR (areas related to reward and emotional arousal – Bryson Lochte and colleagues).

Other research suggests that ASMR-sensitive individuals differ from ASMR-insensitive individuals in terms of their personality, empathy and resting state brain activity (Beverley Fredborg and colleagues; Janik McErlean and Michael Banissy; Stephen Smith and colleagues). For example, those who experience ASMR are thought to be more open to experience, have more empathetic concern for others, and may be less able to inhibit their sensory–emotional responses.

ASMR research is in its infancy and, of course, much more research needs to be conducted to develop a mature science of ASMR. Nevertheless, we are at an immensely exciting period for this emerging field. What makes ASMR research particularly special is the involvement, interest and insight from the ASMR community (those who experience and/or practise ASMR). I'm always touched when people take the time to contact me about their experience, share insights and offer to take part in research.

Above all, I'm incredibly grateful to ASMRtists like Emma, who is truly an expert in her field. ASMRtists not only dedicate significant amounts of time and energy to their videos for the benefit of hundreds and thousands of viewers, but they have also unwittingly provided research materials (through videos, viewer comments and personal insights). Emma in particular has championed ASMR research and spread awareness of our findings in a way that we could never have achieved through academic publications alone. My hope is that researchers, members of the ASMR community and others will come together to drive a collaborative research agenda that examines the positive contribution that ASMR makes to our lives. I know that Emma's insights here will encourage and guide others to discover the potential benefits and power of ASMR.

Dr Giulia Poerio, PhD MSc
Department of Psychology, University of Essex, UK

PART 1

More Than A Feeling

Chapter 1

What is ASMR?

ASMR is primarily the name for a physical sensation. It is sometimes described by experiencers as 'tingles' or 'sparkles'. This tingly sensation usually begins on the scalp and often then travels down the back and through the limbs. However, there are many varying accounts as to how it occurs for different people. At times I have noticed it begin in random areas of the body and either travel from that point or simultaneously happen in lots of places. In the head it can sometimes begin in a little spot that we might unknowingly mistake for an itch. Once we scratch, it could then either intensify or disappear. At other times it might quickly rush all over the whole head. Similarly, in the body we can feel it all over or in just a single place. Again, it can be slow and creeping or there can be an intense rush everywhere. I have even known people say they surprisingly only felt it in their left elbow, a knee or one foot. Overall the general consensus among those who discuss it is that it's a tingly sensation and it can be experienced in many different ways.

To me it feels wonderful. Many people use the word 'euphoria' when they talk about it, which to me is a more emotional and 'elating' description. I find myself always coming back to the word 'sparkles' in my attempt to describe the physical sensation. If I had to use a sound to explain the initial feeling, it would be like crinkling plastic, popping candy or crackling rice cereal. Or if you put some bicarbonate of soda onto the palm of your hand and then added a drop or two of water and felt it bubble against your skin. Now imagine that feeling beneath your skin and inside your body and you're close – it's like pins and needles, but a really pleasant version. What follows soon after the sparkles is a total stillness, a heavy and grounded feeling in the body, almost as if all the tensions in the body are released and the sparkles take over. The mind tends to empty, or at least becomes clearer, and we arrive into a beautiful relaxed state or daydream.

Variety in response

We all experience life from our own perspective, our own 'window' according to what has led us to the point we are at now. The same goes for ASMR. There seem to be lots of factors involved in how intensely we feel it and what we respond to – factors such as where we are when it happens to us, how comfortable or relaxed we are, or how we are feeling in other ways at the time and if we are even open to experiencing it in the first place.

Some people feel it, note it, but don't think of it as anything important and ignore it. Over time this can result in them not experiencing it fully again, as if they have trained themselves out of it. I have heard that medication numbs it for some. Even the temperature in the room can have an effect on the intensity. Many people say that when they discover particular ASMR videos on YouTube they feel it more intensely everywhere and in places they have never felt it before.

Anecdotal evidence seems to show that there are two different types of ASMR experience: the first, Type A, is when we can decide ourselves to feel it, usually through visualisation and memory. And secondly, Type B, when we require an external source in order to experience it – such as a 'whispering video'; watching someone perform an intricate, methodical task; or close-up personal attention. We're going to look at all types of experiences in this book, and particularly at how we can learn to prompt ourselves to feel the 'tingles' or the deep state of relaxation that comes along with it, and then to develop and deepen the sensation. Many people have only known or seen ASMR through YouTube videos, but there is a huge world of ASMR sensation out there that is open to those who can explore their sensitivity and learn how to harness it.

Not everyone experiences this specific feeling. For example, my husband and daughter don't feel it but my son and I do. I have spoken to so many people in my adult life since learning its name. I've become pretty good at explaining it by now and I can tell a whole room full of people about it. Not everyone will recognise what I'm talking about, but what is wonderful is that the people who feel it understand in just a sentence or two. Their eyes immediately light up and they say, 'Yes, I get that!' It's always followed by, 'There's a name for it?' It's so special to witness that realisation in other people and to be able to tell them something about themselves they might not have previously understood, something that they can also now share with others.

Sensitives

We are just starting to explore the science behind this, but my experience is that it's usually more sensitive people who feel it, those veering towards the 'HSP' (Highly Sensitive Person) personality type. People who don't experience it, or are not attracted to it, tend to be less bothered by loud sounds, bright lights or a picture out of place on a wall, for instance. They can generally sleep for a longer period and not be woken by sounds around them or annoyed by a ticking clock; they're maybe not so much of a 'details' person. Perhaps they even find comfort in loud sounds, so living on a busy road would be fine for them as they like a lot of activity and bustle. Sensitive people with a heightened awareness of everything happening around them often struggle with these things, or at least feel and notice them more. Coping with them is a skill for some.

That's not to say that people who don't experience the ASMR sensation are not sensitive at all and cannot benefit from these tools and techniques. They definitely will; thousands do – they are just sensitive to different things. Similarly there are people who still identify as sensitive, an empath or an HSP yet don't specifically feel the tingles, but they feel other positive effects.

When we learn about the name ASMR or become aware of these feelings, many people begin to recall stories from childhood of their 'first' experiences and when they remember noticing it. Often these experiences start from the age of about four or five, when we are said to become fully self-aware. These memories are usually based around nurturing practices, perhaps having our hair played with or brushed, letters 'drawn' on our back, tracing down our arms. Being read a story at bedtime, or a teacher leaning over us at school to look at our work and explaining something calmly and quietly in a gentle voice.

Other situations are more sound-based. These could be hearing other pupils sorting pencils in class, the clicking sound of playing with marbles in the playground or lying in bed at night and listening to rain fall on the roof. I once received a lovely email from a viewer telling me about an experience that really stood out to her from childhood: she was with her grandma visiting a haberdashery store and was able to recall every detail about the visit from start to finish, including the soft voice of the lady serving them, the sound of the buttons as they were sorted into little piles, and the picking out, measuring and snipping of material. It was lovely to read, even an ASMR experience in itself.

How it all began

Back in October 2007 there appeared a comment on a website called steadyhealth.com from an account named 'okaywhatever51838'. It begins: 'I get this sensation sometimes. there's no real trigger for it. it just happens randomly. it's been happening since I was a kid and I'm 21 now.' Many replies were received and a discussion began. This was the birth of the online ASMR community.

Later, more online discussions began elsewhere, including a website and a Yahoo group. Then on 26 March 2009 – my favourite part of this story – a video appeared on YouTube titled 'Whisper 1 – hello!' It was uploaded by 'WhisperingLife', a young lady from the Midlands in England. The description read: 'I know this might sound really weird to some, but I love hearing people whisper! So I thought I would make a whispering channel.' This went on to inspire a whole community of 'whisperers', all making content for each other to induce the feeling everyone was enjoying and becoming more and more curious about. Then, around early 2010 and after much conversation, an ASMR hero and woman-on-a-mission, East Coast US-based Jennifer Allen finally gave the feeling a name. Jennifer had been part of the earlier discussion on steadyhealth. com and she had decided to open a Facebook group, and then later founded asmr-research.org. 'A' was for Autonomous – meaning it happens on its own, 'automatically'; 'S' for Sensory, as it is a physical sensation; 'M' for Meridian, from Chinese medicine (and acupuncture), where it means a system of pathways around the body which energy is said to flow; and 'R' for Response, as it is primarily a reaction to something. ASMR was born.

'We are all just walking each other home.'

Ram Dass

What's in a name?

Giving this feeling a name was absolutely key to spreading awareness. It facilitated much faster growth of the online community, encouraged conversation and theories about it and made describing it so much easier. Whisper videos increased in popularity and more people began creating content on YouTube.

It was then possible for scientific research to begin. University research departments quickly became interested; not surprisingly, many of the researchers are experiencers themselves. The first scientific paper to be published on ASMR was from the Department of Psychology at Swansea University in Wales in March 2015, titled 'Autonomous Sensory Meridian Response (ASMR): A Flow-like Mental State'. Emma Barratt and Nick Davis interviewed nearly 500 participants and showed that ASMR definitely existed and that people utilised it for self-help. It immediately showed certain commonalities: the most usual 'triggers' for ASMR were whispering (in 75 per cent of interviewees) and 'personal attention' (in 69 per cent of interviewees), and the majority of people used it before bed (81 per cent).

The next prominent scientific study, the first of its kind from Sheffield University in England, was titled 'More Than a Feeling: Autonomous Sensory Meridian Response (ASMR) is characterised by reliable changes in affect and physiology' by Giulia Poerio, Thomas Hostler, Emma Blakey and Theresa Veltri. They found that while viewing ASMR online content, ASMR-sensitive viewers' heart rates declined considerably in line with meditation techniques. Also, there was an increase in skin conductivity or 'galvanic skin response'

– meaning that electrical conductivity increased, suggesting a more intense emotional response during the experience.

Other studies have taken place around the world, including an fMRI study in the US finding that various brain regions are significantly activated during the experience. Another in Canada showed that ASMR and mindfulness are very much related. I have no doubt that there is much more to come.

The Bob Ross effect

Whisper videos soon became ASMR videos – online content made specifically with the intention to induce the sensation in the viewer. An ASMRtist is someone who creates those videos. However, before these came about, and well before the first whisper video was made, there were many people watching certain TV programmes or listening to sounds that gave them the sensation. Have you ever heard of a man named Bob Ross? If you're from the US then the chances are that you have. Bob was an artist, art teacher and TV host in the 1980s – he created and hosted *The Joy of Painting*, which aired in the US and also in Latin America, Canada and some parts of Europe. He is now lovingly called the 'godfather of ASMR'. His calm manner, soft voice and the kind way he had of describing his painting techniques, along with his little quirky but insightful expressions here and there and the sounds his brushes made on the canvas, made him the perfect tingle provider, paternal figure and, many say, guru.

'As long as you are learning, you're not failing.'

Bob Ross

Shopping channels were also regularly frequented, as were unintentionally calming tutorials on YouTube. For me I loved *The Antiques Roadshow* and lying on the sofa on a Sunday listening to the sounds of a snooker tournament play out on the TV. In fact I happened to feel it more from TV on a Sunday, when all was calm around me and the day slower.

Others refer to 'Mister Rogers' as being an ASMR legend – the beloved children's TV presenter in the US who hosted the show *Mister Rogers' Neighborhood* which aired from 1968 to 2001. Carefully building things while singing and chatting along, his calm voice and genuine warmth is ASMR personified.

Tingling into popular culture

By the time I joined the ASMR community, the community was growing faster and gaining momentum. It was still very small, especially compared to what it is now, but people were aware of its existence and they were situated all over the world. Just as I became aware of the name for my feeling through searching online, others were doing the same every day – like light bulbs switching on all over the world. Some would dive straight in through YouTube, commenting and sharing straight away; others preferred to watch without signing up for an account and stay anonymous. I say it like this was a long time ago (it really wasn't), but many people thought that ASMR videos were slightly weird or, if they didn't think they were odd, they straight away assumed they might be a fetish or for sexual gratification. It was still difficult to explain. I know many viewers who could not tell their partners, family, friends or work colleagues that they watched ASMR videos or experienced ASMR for fear others would not understand. They also didn't really know how to put into words what they were feeling anyway.

When the phrase 'brain orgasm' started to be used in the press, it conjured up a whole host of connotations. These articles didn't help but, on the other hand, the sensationalism really made people look and think for themselves. For every article explaining it in whatever way they wanted, there were people reading it or sending it to their friends and recognising the feeling they had experienced all their lives. For those who do experience it, they know it isn't a sexual or a weird thing and ASMR is now firmly placed in the wellness space. And thank goodness for that! I for one was getting tired of answering the 'is it sexual?' question in interviews and the constant battle to normalise what is just a natural, non-sexual feeling that has likely been experienced since the dawn of time. As they say, people mock what they don't understand.

I am a mother, so it especially became a mission of mine to speak about it as much as I could in the most positive way, to explain its comforting and nurturing qualities, and to make videos that others would be comfortable to use as a tool to explain it to their friends, family or partners.

Good news travels fast. Through the growing popularity of videos, ASMRtists talking in interviews in the media, comedians and celebrities talking about it on TV, social-media sharing and more Facebook groups, it became the online phenomenon it is today. Brands have also taken on the techniques used in videos and applied them to their advertising, the most famous at the moment being the 2019 Super Bowl beer advert. Some have hired ASMRtists to make adverts, put on events or record content like mini-films or a podcast. Opinions about this sort of thing differ within the community, and not surprisingly so. ASMR started off as a small community of people connecting online, united in common interests, becoming friends and partners and comforting each other through an escape from the stresses and pressures of life. For everyone who experiences it, it's a beautiful and exciting discovery based around a lovely physical sensation, often with strong and nostalgic child-hood memories attached. We're now seeing it 'used' by the commercial world and sometimes perhaps it is attached to a brand that represents almost the opposite of what ASMR is about. However, when a brand comes to it through similarities in purpose or ethos, the two worlds can complement each other well.

Every year thousands – now becoming millions – of people all over the world find out more about them-selves, become more self-aware and potentially learn to use ASMR as a tool for wellbeing. All because of the *whole* of the ASMR movement, not just one aspect of it. I should also add that more awareness also brings more funding for scientific research, which, as we have seen so far, is beneficial for everyone. Not just the sensation experiencers but for others who we are finding the tech-niques can help with stress relief, anxiety, concentration, pain relief or simple relaxation.

In this current climate where likes, shares, subscrib-ers, statistics and branding are seen as important and a benchmark for success, the more popular ASMR is then the more people – and most importantly, youngsters – can show it to their peers as something they experience or are interested in without fear of being judged or misun-derstood. I know this because when my channel started to grow, my children got fewer comments from school about what their mum does online and more impressed reactions. I also received less ridicule on TV and in the press. Apart from I suppose improved lighting and make-up skills, I wasn't making content any differently from before, it was just being viewed differently.

WHAT ISN'T ASMR?

Admittedly at first glance it's hard to tell by looking online. ASMR has become so popular all over the world and has been merged with so many other online phenomena, styles and trends. The general opinion has come to be that no one is really allowed to say what it isn't. As it is a personal experience, and everyone feels it slightly differently, it would be non-inclusive to tell others what is and isn't their ASMR. However, to me ASMR is nothing that doesn't have heart and soul in it. That is to say, there should be kindness and nurturing in it somewhere. So I see no ASMR, for example, in a video of someone throwing items like pencils or dinner plates into a huge shredder. But sitting quietly with the viewer, taking time to be still while slowly rolling your hands over a row of pencils or gently tapping on the plates, perhaps tracing the patterns on them, creating a calming sound and with interesting immersive visuals, would be ASMR.

As ASMR videos became more popular – and YouTube after all is an arm of the Google algorithm – then using the term in the title of a video gets more views. So in short: 'Look at my boobies, I'm eating ants while talking about cats and sitting in the world's biggest pizza ASMR' is likely to receive more attention quickly and be moved up the video rankings compared to 'Sitting with you and calmly tapping ASMR'. Emergence of the internet and the digital era has been vital in the communication of and awareness of ASMR, but undoubtedly there is a side serving of a downside. But ASMR is not 'just' about sound, just about a feeling, just about only one thing at all – it's complex and about lots of things together.

A new complementary therapy

ASMR is something for all living beings on the planet: people of all ages, all backgrounds, all geographical locations and all genders. People of all differences can be touched positively by it. (Animals love ASMR too. I have pictures of many animals sitting transfixed by my videos.) The point is ASMR transcends everything and is universal. It is wonderful and exciting to learn about the physiological effects on our bodies and have our theories or knowing explored by science. Further studies will be vitally important, but it's been equally exciting to be a part of something unknown and in its infancy as far as mainstream science and the collective consciousness of people is concerned.

For me, and I know for many others, this is a lesson in acceptance for things we might not initially understand and a new way of thinking. No matter what our background, current conditioning, state of health, personal interests, beliefs, anything, we still share the desire to be healthy, happy, calm, connected and still. We're all humans living on the same planet trying our best to live fully, live well, or even just survive day to day, within our body and immediate environment.

Chapter 2

My Story

Before I tell you how ASMR could possibly help you in your life, perhaps I ought to tell you how it helped me. This is how ASMR changed my life.

I was born in the seventies; my dad was a builder and my mum a nurse. I'm the oldest of three, with a younger sister and brother. Over time I became a responsible big sister, albeit a bit bossy and I didn't like it when they messed up my room, but I was kind, fun and patient. Outside of the home, I remember being told to 'speak up' a lot by adults and that I was 'shy'. I would always put others' needs before my own. Now I realise I was just extremely sensitive, inward-thinking and easily embarrassed, but as a child I remember feeling confused and frustrated often. The outside world didn't seem to match my inside world. My inner world was colourful and full of thoughts and I had a vivid imagination, but expressing that to others was difficult. My days were very sensory – I noticed, heard and felt everything around me and would think about it over and over again afterwards. On the whole I was a happy soul but life felt overwhelming sometimes, and as a child I didn't have the tools or understanding to deal with it properly.

On the outside I was a smiley, 'good' and mostly quiet girl; I loved to be alone, thinking, rearranging my room, sorting through things and daydreaming.

An ASMR story

Many of my teachers at primary school were extremely strict and unkind, to the point where pretending to be ill became a skill for me. So when one year I found myself in a class with a lovely, gentle teacher, you can imagine – it was the best year ever. I still remember her now. Carpet time was amazing; her calm voice when reading us stories coupled with other students playing with my hair or tracing patterns on my back was magical. I used to feel a sparkly sensation all through my head and down my back. My body would become heavy and I felt sleepy and daydreamy. This is a feeling I was very familiar with. I didn't know what it was, if it had a name or if anyone else experienced it, it was just there and part of my normal sensory experience of life. I assumed everyone 'had' it.

Later on, I developed Bell's palsy, which set me apart from the other children. It makes half of your face paralysed and takes a while to recover from, if you ever do. I still have a wonky smile and generally uneven face.

Later, after moving schools and being the new, shy kid, I became the target of regular bullying. So being different was something I became used to but I also had the sense that I *felt* differently about things than other people did. So I'd ask questions about this 'sparkly' feeling. Pain, sadness, happiness, warmth, coldness and pins and needles are all physical sensations or feelings we are taught a name for, but not this one. My questions just got me a blank look, so I stopped talking about it. It was my comfort and a self-soothing tool, something I could trigger for myself with visualisation or by picking out sounds in my environment.

As a teen I became more feisty and brave. As someone who noticed and mentally documented everyone else's behaviour around me, I was good at upsetting the apple cart by pointing out the truth or calling people out. I learned to internalise again and became frustrated but quite angry this time. Life has always been an emotional rollercoaster.

One thing I learned on this eventful journey of mine was that the strongest of us are those who have struggled, survived and come out of it all smiling. They emerge more compassionate and brave enough to move forward with a purpose. To remain positive and hopeful when life has been difficult is a hard task indeed and if you're one of these people I am proud of you. If you've had a terrible time of it but remain a grumpy old thing, then I can't say I blame you one bit! Be kind to yourself.

It seems that in order to wake up, change our way of thinking, look at the path we are on and make positive changes in life, often something has to happen: a traumatic event to shift us off our timeline, a near miss, a gentle nudge or a painful episode of some kind. My 'something' happened in December 2010.

I was dashing around in my own world. Fast-forward from the sensitive young girl: I was now a mum of two young children, wife, keeper of a home we could barely afford that needed total renovation, and ran two small businesses. I was exhausted, overwhelmed and distracted a lot of the time. I was everyone's 'yes' person and champion people-pleaser. Home life was often tricky. My husband and I worked so hard, we were tired and had little patience left by the end of each day. We have always had a deep connection, love and understanding for one another but once we settled down together and, very early on, started a family, responsibility hit us like a tonne of bricks. Getting along day to day became difficult. Suddenly everything that each of us needed to process and work on from our early lives came up to bite us. There is nothing like pressure, tiredness and a tight budget to test one's character and relationship.

Then, in December 2010, with snow on the ground and Christmas coming, I was at work with two sick children beside me, on a tight deadline and tired from another big argument at home the night before. The phone was ringing all day and with another large pile of washing looming, I was also trying to pack up to move out of our home the next day for renovations to begin. While on my way to run an errand, along came a car and scooped me up onto the bonnet. I looked into the eyes of the driver and all I could feel was a helpless, disappointed feeling followed by total surrender. 'Typical,' I thought to myself. We travelled down the road for what seemed like forever, until finally I lost my grip, fell off into the snow on the side of the road and blacked out.

My injuries resulted in a long stay in hospital over Christmas, a full leg plaster, several operations, then a wheelchair, crutches and physiotherapy. The worst thing was the absolute agony of needing other people to take over my responsibilities for me. Not being able to take care of my children was awful. I've always been a mum on a mission, and them being so young they needed me such a lot. At least I was alive, I told myself: 'Thank goodness for that, I have too much to do!'

Believe it or not, this event proved to be the best thing that could have happened to me. The car stopped me in my tracks. It quite literally woke me up. I had to rebuild my life bit by bit: friends, family, living situation, work, relationship with my husband, the way I thought of and treated myself. Seeing my life from another perspective shed light on relationships and behaviours that were counterproductive. Suddenly I realised that I wasn't a machine and everyone else's caretaker, that the happiness

I was aiming for in life wasn't going to come from living the way I was. In fact I was caught in a vicious cycle of behaviour. Through trying to be everything to everyone I wasn't only making things worse for myself but for everyone else too.

That's not to say the process was quick. My emotional, physical and mental development after that day was long and at times extremely painful. For me it was a matter of handing back responsibility to others who had caused me pain. Also handing others practical responsibilities for things I had always done for them but really they should be doing for themselves. It was removing myself from relationships with others that were unhealthy, not making allowances for others any longer and making space for me to prioritise my daily life and take better care of myself. Learning more self-respect too.

Changing your environment can take a long time, especially when it involves other people, and even longer if it involves your location or living situation – not just for practical reasons but emotional ones too. You need little reminders and signs to keep you on track. Significant events can come up and remind you of why you decided to change. At times you may slip backwards and find yourself behaving as you used to. Perhaps you need therapy to talk it though and learn coping techniques. It's relearning how to live and learning about the new you from this awakened perspective.

A sprinkling of stardust

Along this bumpy road something rather magical happened for me. It was as significant as the car accident in a really good way and I have never been the same again.

In November 2012, after most of the operations were done, I was walking again and supposedly 'back to normal', but unbeknownst to me at that time I was dealing with severe PTSD symptoms. Depression, panic attacks, disassociation and sleeplessness were my normal state of being. At the time I just assumed I was tired and needed a break, but we were too busy and couldn't afford it anyway. I'd not that long had a smartphone and so I decided to download the YouTube app. I thought perhaps I'd find relaxation videos on there to help me fall asleep. Years ago, in my early twenties, I would regularly fall asleep to old cassette tapes of *The Goon Show* or recordings of other old radio shows, so I started off my search with 'rainforest sounds', then 'nature sounds' and meditations. It took a few nights and I'm not sure how it happened, but soon enough I began to notice 'ASMR' this or that come up in the search suggestions. I remember ignoring them a few times before finally clicking on one. Even then I didn't really understand what was going on there. After a while though I stumbled on a few that made sense. They were relaxing to watch and made me feel calm. One in particular stood out to me. It was a kind-looking woman with a soft voice sitting in a very tidy and low-lit, cosy room. She said she had a sweet in her mouth for 'extra sounds' and while listening and looking around the room she was in and wondering who she was, the lovely feeling came back to me. Slowly I put two and two together. ASMR was the name for my feeling. Not only was there a name, but other people experienced it too, in other countries, and they were talking about it online. The joy I felt was truly wonderful and from that moment on I was hooked. Who was the kind lady? My now dear friend, Maria Gentle Whispering.

ASMR videos became my new online sanctuary. I could experience my lovely familiar feeling ten-fold, whenever I wanted to. Feeling it again so often caused me to remember experiences from my childhood, where I was, what I was doing, how lovely it was. It caused me to question everything: what it was, why I felt it and others not; what was going on in my body physically during this experience? How am I similar to the people I'm watching on YouTube? What is it about us that perhaps is different? How is it that we experience it all over the world regardless of any other differences?

I didn't have an account and would never comment but I would read all the comments below the videos, studying everything that people said, their opinions, how open they were, what ideas and stories they had. This new world was fascinating to me and the people in it were angels. I had a lot of favourite channels to watch at that time – many of them don't upload any more, sadly, but some of their videos are still there for me to pop back and reminisce at. Every new upload was exciting and a gift for me. Again I decided to talk to other people around me about it and did this with great excitement. Again I was met with total bewilderment or just, 'Oh, that's nice,' so I kept it to myself again and it became my own little haven. A tool for self-soothing, my own little world. Only now it was much bigger than before. 'Thank goodness for the internet,' I thought.

Through my regular use of ASMR, aside from the gift of learning more about myself – self-realisation, just at a time when I was experiencing issues – I found I became calm more regularly, felt more centred and, most of all, I was sleeping much better. The ASMR experience through watching videos was very intense for me at the time. I felt that in a way it recalibrated me before bedtime, calming me down and helping me to stop thinking about things I couldn't do anything about at that time of night. The sleep I was having was better quality than before and I tended to wake up feeling more rested.

A few months passed and along came a video about International ASMR Day in February 2013. It was with Maria and Ilse (Waterwhispers) and they were talking about the ASMR community. The community, even though scattered all over the world, was still quite small then and Ilse suggested that there should be groups formed in each country to bring people together. I of course decided she was talking to me and I was needed, so I opened a Facebook group named ASMR UK (now ASMR UK & Ireland). It was really great to begin communicating with others online about something I'd experienced all my life but couldn't find a way to openly express. An ASMR community member I became. These were my people.

In July 2013 my friend and co-admin at the time for the Facebook group, Shola (Charming ASMR), told me of the first ever ASMR meet-up, in London. It was organised by Ilse and her partner Chris, and it was just for people with an ASMR YouTube channel. I really wanted to go, so I very tentatively opened one. Shola had asked me before what my channel was and it seemed most people had one. It was a way to communicate further and get to know one another properly. Videos would sometimes be about things people collected, what they had done that day, chatting about interests they had and places they lived. A video version of a Facebook account. Filming myself was absolutely nerve-wracking. The first video I uploaded was filmed on the iPad we had for the children, propped up on the bedside table, the wrong way round: 19 July 2013: 'Hello everyone, this is ... er ... my first video. My name is ... er ... Emma, the whispers red. Um ... for my first video I'm going to unbox my brand new video camera.' This video is one minute and twenty-three seconds long. I'd bought said camera on credit from a catalogue and had no idea how to use it, how to edit a video and upload it properly, how to do much at all really.

But that was it, I was officially part of the tribe. An ASMR content creator, a YouTuber and on the list for the meet-up. I went. I was so nervous and excited. Everyone was. So I made myself useful beforehand. I lived in London, so I could help out with an itinerary for everyone, organising places to go, helping out with lifts, generally making sure everyone was happy. What followed was two days of pure excitement. They were a kind and very fun bunch.

After that day my confidence slowly grew. People told me they enjoyed my voice and the sounds I made. It was a challenge to be 'observed', to open myself up to criticism and to see myself in detail on camera. This was a much larger-scale version of trying to explain ASMR to people in conversation and finding they didn't know what I was talking about. This was an expression of ASMR in a very public way with no explanation for those who didn't know what it was. I had intentionally thrown myself completely open with no guarantee that everything would be alright and I wouldn't fall flat on my face. I was finally becoming my true authentic self and everyone around me was just going to have to gossip about it or come to terms with it.

Through making my own videos, communicating online and watching others, I became much more aware of mental health and how the issues we have present themselves. Many videos at that time were quite intimate and we would hear stories from others about their past experiences and therapy they may have had. The community was a lot smaller then than it is today, with fewer people watching and many of them regular commenters. We were all quite close and it was easier to be that open when we were such a small part of YouTube. This made me realise what I was experiencing in my own life, day to day. I recognised the near-constant anxiety I felt, the panic attacks and that I was depressed a lot of the time. Through regularly feeling the ASMR sensation, and noticing it more when it happened during regular activities throughout my days, I was observing myself more and stopping to notice how I was feeling. Not just the good feelings but the bad too. Once this happened I realised I needed help and had the courage to ask for it.

Through our wonderful NHS I got to see a therapist and was diagnosed with severe PTSD. Not only that but as soon as I was diagnosed and told that it wasn't my fault, I completely broke down. With lots of talking, understanding, careful advice and homework from my absolutely amazing therapist, everything changed very quickly. I sailed through the treatment with ASMR as my complementary therapy. Practising self-acceptance, accompanied by the good-quality sleep I was able to achieve, gave me the energy and patience to put the skills I was given into practice so that they would become habit.

The whole world was new for me and my eyes were wide open to the possibilities of happiness, joy and contentment.

Since my introduction to ASMR videos, alongside meeting people from the community in person, it has always been important for me to bring people together if possible. I am a big fan of in-person ASMR techniques, which I have experimented with a lot, so in February 2016 I worked with an artist named Thomas Grogan on a live ASMR session. It was terrifying but wonderful and since then I have gone on to host many events in other countries.

Many children love ASMR. Imagine being aware of this feeling from a young age, and having a name for it – that is awesome to me. In November 2014 I started making ASMR videos aimed at a younger age group because many of my viewers were telling me they watched videos with their children before sleep. I thought they would like to see content around counting, telling the time or playing with sensory items like kinetic sand. It's a beautiful project to work on and the feedback has been absolutely lovely and encouraging.

Then in 2015 I embarked on a two-year course in sound healing. So many people had said 'you are helping me', 'you're a healer', or 'these videos are healing for me' and I wanted to understand more. I'd always been interested in complementary therapies and had seen a reiki therapist in the past. The session had been a profound experience. I wanted to learn how alternative methods that were more advanced and accepted by society could compare to what was happening with ASMR, to see if any of the techniques were similar and if perhaps I could use them to enhance the ASMR experience. I saw that there were other relaxation healing methods and I chose sound healing as I thought it was the most similar to ASMR. It was another tool in my belt for self-growth. I now understood how important the voice is for connection with others and how sound can be used as a tool for wellbeing (I'll talk more about this later). Later I completed courses in crystal and Himalayan singing bowls, assemblage point healing (which is fascinating) and reiki. In the future, when I have the time, I'd love to learn aromatherapy and massage techniques.

Sometimes I agree to work with brands, depending on what they're selling of course. As ASMR has become more popular online there are more companies who want to align themselves with its popularity or feel that what it represents works with their brand or intentions. It's fun to get out there and raise awareness and as long as I feel it brings something to the table in terms of enhancing the ASMR experience, I'm happy with that.

These days, at times I am busier than I have ever been in my whole life. However, I am now a much calmer and more attentive mother to my children. Through my experiences I have been able to teach them so much more than I would have done if I hadn't been stopped by that car, found ASMR and had therapy. We have our moments of drama just like any family but together we are stronger, communication is important, and we talk things through and are open with one another. My husband and I have worked through such a lot, together and separately. We're now able to support each other to be the best we can be, have more patience and work together as a team. He is the most supportive person I have ever met. We do have our moments and we disagree, but letting go is so much easier now because there is no underlying resentment about things from the past. Well, mostly anyway – we're human after all. Overall, and most importantly, my awakening became theirs and we're all better for it.

Sometimes, when life is uncomfortable, you feel something is wrong but you're not sure what it is, or a problem doesn't seem big enough to do anything about, it is easier to just leave things as they are. But being brave enough to go through the pain and period of chaos can result in a life you never imagined.

I still get stressed now and then, and I also have plenty of moments of self-doubt and emotional challenge. It's hard to put yourself 'out there' online, but I know my limits and it's a different type of stress. The other one, the old 'stress', was more of a lost, confused, worn-out and helpless feeling. I know now that I'm on the right path. I understand that we're all on a journey and are here to experience and learn. My job is to be the best I can be from the inside out, to help others, whenever I am able, to be as calm as they can be in order to do the same. To walk their own path. I'm just here to give Love.

This is how ASMR changed my life. It's been a life-changing discovery for many others. I hope it can be a positive part of your story too.

Chapter 3

The Language of ASMR

The ASMR sensation occurs in response to what is called a 'trigger'. The list of potential triggers is vast and varied, and everyone who experiences or enjoys ASMR tends to have their own set of preferred triggers. What may be a strong stimulus for one person may not be for another. We don't know exactly why that is yet.

There have been plenty of theories discussed throughout the community online regarding different types of trigger. There was even a study that suggested certain personality traits are more attracted to particular types of stimuli. Perhaps certain triggers are just more suitable for the feeling itself, physiologically speaking? Once we know more about what happens in the body during the response, that might help us understand the connections. I believe we all have different preferences according to our experiences, upbringings and current life situations. We might need, for example, a certain nurturing at a particular time. We also just have our natural preferences as individuals, and I feel this informs our responses, just as with our tastes in food and music.

Types of trigger

ASMR stimuli can generally be split into four different categories in order to best explain them: Sound, Touch, Visual and Personal Attention – though there are natural overlaps between them. There are also consistencies throughout the different types, in that they all arrive or are delivered softly. Whether it's touch, sound or visual in action, the trigger is usually gentle and comforting – it isn't too loud or in a tone that aggravates or could cause discomfort. It is also always delivered with good intention – the warmth and nurturing qualities of ASMR are a huge part of its ability to bring comfort and to encourage safety and companionship in the receiver.

ASMR stimuli are usually connected to nature and nurture also – whether it's hair-brushing or gentle rainfall, we instinctively find reassurance and contentment in sounds and actions that take us back to our beginnings and that naturally tap into the nostalgia of happy, often slower, times – childhood pastimes, lazy Sundays, feeling safe with loved ones.

Triggers can be experienced in two different ways. They can be intentionally 'given' by someone – in person or through a video/recording – or they can occur naturally during our day-to-day lives. It is a common misconception, especially upon first discovery of ASMR, that it is defined by video content only. This is just one way to communicate and experience it. What we will explore in Chapters 5 and 6, and later in Part 2 of the book, is how you can create your own triggers and how you can learn to experience ASMR in your usual, every-day life activities.

The categories, examples and descriptions of common triggers is ever-expanding; however they all have basic similarities. Perhaps you are familiar with some of these triggers and already associate them with a comforting feeling, or perhaps they are all new to you. I hope there is something interesting here for those at all stages of ASMR awareness.

Sound

Sound is a very important aspect of the most popular triggers for ASMR. The voice, sounds *from* objects, *with* objects, and nature and nurture sounds all form a base for a full ASMR experience. They can be purposefully delivered or occur naturally, and can be rhythmic, slow, a little fast or in an ad-hoc motion – however, they are always soft.

The voice

For me the most important aspect of ASMR is the voice. Our voices are powerful, and the sound of our voice is a language in itself, sometimes regardless of the words you use (which we will talk about again later).

There are many different vocal triggers in ASMR – they are used both in videos and in 'in-person' sessions with others. The most frequent vocal triggers include whispering or speaking softly or a mixture of the two, with emphasis on the top frequencies ('swhispering' feels like a nice word for that), along with mouth sounds made with a light use of voice.

There is also what is called 'rambling' in ASMR, which is softly speaking at a regular pace about something with no particular story to it. This could be anything that doesn't require too much attention from the listener, like talking about a nail polish collection or what someone bought at the supermarket that day perhaps. It is not an in-depth topic or story that needs to be followed or requires concentration.

We can also use the voice to tell a detailed story about something very personal. This requires the listener to be fully immersed and follow along with their imagination, which is a different type of trigger, and a more thorough distraction from our personal thoughts.

ASMR also often uses a disconnected voice, so that the personality of the person speaking or whispering is taken out of the scenario – such as when the ASMRtist is reading someone else's words, like text on a product bottle for example. Think about when we read a book out loud and how our voice takes on a different pitch, speed and perhaps rhythm as if we 'deliver' the words.

This is very different than if we were directly communicating by asking someone if they would like a cup of tea, which naturally brings in more of our personality and has a completely different sound to it.

Similar to rambling, unintelligible speaking or whispering is hugely popular in ASMR videos. This is using the voice to make speaking sounds but not saying any words at all. The mouth moves and sound is made but no content is formed, usually only the starting and ending sound of a word. This is very quiet, and again it gives the impression of whispering or talking quietly but removes any actual words that can distract the listener or require their attention.

Speaking in a foreign language works as an ASMR voice trigger in the same way. If the language is not your own and you can't understand the content, you are left to just enjoy the speech flow without becoming immersed in the subject matter or story. Lastly, and probably most importantly, the voice is used as a trigger to convey emotion and intention, which again we will explore later.

Human-made electrical items

The usual man-made items that produce triggering sounds could be a room fan, facial steamer, aromatherapy diffuser or even your refrigerator or washing machine at home. I remember I was answering emails at my kitchen table once and suddenly my head started tingling. I focused to listen for what had triggered it, as I assumed at first that it was my typing on the keyboard. The room at that time was very quiet and there weren't any sounds from outside, but I realised that the refrigerator had just kicked in and started whirring. It was nice. Sometimes I feel it from the sound of an aeroplane in the distance too.

WHAT IS FRISSON?

This is an emotional physical response to music or the excited anticipatory feeling we get when something is about to happen. It can sometimes be misinterpreted as ASMR tingles when you are explaining it, as it seems more people know this feeling than experience ASMR. It is quite different altogether. Frisson is a sudden rush of feeling that comes and goes quite quickly. It is also exciting and keeps us alert whereas ASMR is longer-lasting, slower and results in more of a sleepy feeling than an excited or aroused one.

Sounds with objects

This is often deliberately using or 'playing' an object by tapping or scratching it with the fingerpads or nails. You could try a tool, but it is more personal and triggering to observe someone use their hands directly. These different objects could be made from materials that generate different sounds – like wood, stone, plastic bottles or glass. They may be solid or hollow and they create different depths of sound in the same way wooden musical instruments do. In fact I like to think that any object can become an instrument.

Other common sound triggers are from using the object, e.g. turning the pages of a book, cutting different materials, unboxing a package, opening and closing lids, writing or colouring with pencils or pens (which is particularly interesting given the recent interest in adult colouring-in as a calming pastime), opening a crinkly packet or typing on a keyboard. There are so many naturally occurring scenarios here – and the best way to find your own personal favourites is to observe what types of sounds make you feel something positive as you go about your normal day, handling a range of materials and 'hearing' objects around you.

Nature triggers

These could be rain on a window or dripping on the ground, trees rustling, a soft wind, birdsong, a bee buzzing outside the window, or crunching leaves beneath the feet. They can also be sounds made *with* nature like peeling fruit, chopping an apple, playing with cacao beans or dried flowers, lentils or dried beans (and the accompanying physical touch sensation). You can also use items that are made from nature – simple wooden instruments or shakers. Food or personal care items from nature that create sounds, like bubbles, the crackle of foam or trickle of oils, also resonate strongly. It's as though sounds can be more comforting if they are directly from or are made with something natural or from Mother Nature.

'Nature is our church.' —Björk

Nurture sounds

Nurture is a very important trigger. A sound reminiscent of being cared for is hugely powerful. This could be quiet singing accompanied by the sound of soft breath and the sounds that naturally come from the mouth when doing this, similar to singing a lullaby to a child or the rhythmic music patterns that we gravitate towards when we are rocking a baby. It could be something as abstract as the sounds of clothing swishing as a person moves slowly, jewellery tinkling as it sways or smoothing down material.

Skin sounds from hands gliding over each other, like when applying hand cream or carefully rubbing the face, are also soothing and promote feelings of safety and comfort. Gently move your finger over your ear now or stroke your own hand close to your ear and you will hear this sound. Of course nurture sounds are enhanced when delivered in a kind and caring way, a *loving* way.

WHAT IS SYNESTHESIA?

Synesthesia occurs when two senses work simultaneously, one sense being activated at the same time as another. There are many different combinations of this – such as a person who can 'hear' colours or 'see' sounds. One example is mirror-touch synesthesia, where a person is able to 'feel' the sensation of another person being touched as if it is happening to them (in the same way many of us feel pain when another is hurt). Mirror-touch synesthesia is sometimes described as a heightened level of empathy.

WHAT IS MISOPHONIA?

Misophonia is the opposite to ASMR, and sometimes listed as a type of synesthesia. It is a negative 'hatred' response – including negative emotions, thoughts and physical reactions – to certain sounds, for example 'nails on a chalkboard'. It often occurs in those sensitive to ASMR, which is to be expected. If you are sensitive then you are likely to be sensitive to both good and bad sensations.

The level of reaction depends on how severe the person has it or how loud or bad the sound. Misophonia triggers can include loud eating, slurping, wet mouth sounds, sharp 's' sounds when whispering, cutlery sounds on a plate, sniffing, popping gum, slamming doors, heavy walking and many more. The experiencer can feel intense anger or anxiety or both in response.

Since ASMR includes visual triggers also, I should point out that there is another opposite to ASMR, which is misokinesia. This is the hatred of certain visual stimuli and it often accompanies misophonia. Examples of triggers for this are said to be leg-tapping or shaking, swaying and fidgeting, and repetitive movements around the face such as finger-tapping and hair-twisting. Even moving hanging signs or bags swaying can prompt this. It is very difficult for some and that, coupled with a sound for misophonia sufferers, is excruciating. I must admit I feel a bit uncomfortable just writing about it as I experience that too!

Touch

Touch is a language all on its own. We will explore this further in the coming chapters but the main touch triggers are when another person touches you, or as you touch yourself for self-soothing. The touch can be on skin or through material or clothes, with or without tools.

Touch triggers on the back are one of my personal favourites – drawing patterns with the fingerpads or nails, tracing words or pictures in a particular order or ad-hoc motion. This is a very common trigger remembered from childhood – children often naturally 'write' on another child's back and have fun guessing shapes and letters. Of course it's much easier to have someone do this for you, but a light pressure with a back-scratching tool could be used. (I even saw a video online where a person had attached a hand made out of card to a stick coming out of an oscillating fan. He laid down beside it and the fan moved the hand up and down his back. It did make me chuckle and feel secretly envious that I didn't think of it myself!)

Running fingers and nails up and down the inside of the arms where the skin is more sensitive is an intense trigger, as is tracing circles on the palms of the hands. Some areas of the legs and the tops of the feet can be triggering too, although I would say anywhere that is likely to be ticklish should be avoided as the tickle sensation is more annoying or produces an excited feeling that leads more to laughter than relaxation.

These skin triggers can be created using the pads of the fingers or nails – tracing, lightly scratching or tapping. Or they can be made using tools such as a wooden roller, a soft or hard brush (lightly), a comb, a toothbrush, a soft piece of material or a flower even. Anything you find that can be draped or run lightly across the skin. Feathers are nice too – a kind one that was found on the ground and a gift from the sky.

Touch triggers on the face, ears, neck, scalp and hair can produce beautiful tingles and calm. Try gently pulling on small sections of hair, running nails through the hair and across the scalp, lightly scratching the neck and light taps on the forehead or cheeks. Again these can be done using the fingers and nails or with a hairbrush, large make-up brush or anything else you imagine could feel pleasant.

Visual

Immersive visuals can be an important ASMR trigger. They give the eyes and mind something to focus on when the ears and brain are busy taking in sound. Even on their own, with no accompanying sound at all, they can produce a relaxing feeling or the sparkly sensation, especially those produced close up by the hands.

Visual triggers in a video form might be floating hand movements, hands close to the lens of the camera, or objects or hands moving in and out of focus as they move towards and away from the camera. Even visuals like fixating on the mouth of a person as they speak, or watching their eyes or hair move around their shoulders as they do something, can be triggers. We sometimes use colourful light moving slowly around the background and small dots of light moving gently around the screen.

In nature we see effective stimuli in visuals of water ripples, waves going in and out on a sandy beach or watching a snake slither through the desert in a nature programme, trees or shrubs swaying in the breeze or water evaporating from wet stone on a hot day.

At home we might use visual triggers like watching water squeeze out of a sponge in the bath, softly folding fresh dough or smoothing down bedsheets.

WHAT IS SATISFYING ASMR?

Around the summer of 2014 there appeared short ASMR clips from ASMRtists branching out onto a different platform – Vine, then later Facebook and then Instagram – that were satisfying or immersive to look at. These could be clips of ice cream machines churning ice cream, or a time-lapse video of a painting or other piece of art being created – interesting and fun clips of how things are made but that also happened to have pleasant or interesting visuals.

ASMR viewers would share these clips around and say they got tingles from parts of them, or that they couldn't stop watching. After all, lots of these were quite sensory clips too. This seemed to prompt, around the same time, the start of the slime genre of short content, close-up clips of people playing with sensory items like slime or kinetic sand because they are immersive to watch. They became popular and ASMR viewers would sometimes comment under these videos that some of the visuals and sounds were quite like ASMR, so then these creators began using the ASMR tag. This became the 'Satisfying Revolution' and the ASMR tag was used along with it. However, most of these videos don't always utilise ASMR techniques. An immersive visual may work as an ASMR trigger when it is performed gently, and if it is slow or delicate, with soft sounds. Some of these clips are wonderful if the creator really understands ASMR (or is naturally quite a gentle person) and uses the techniques well alongside the satisfying visuals.

Attention-induced triggers

These are similar to visual triggers. Attention-induced tingles are often named as 'watching people do things ASMR' and they are much more immersive than the usual visual triggers. It might be watching someone concentrate deeply on and complete a task from start to finish, such as a carpenter whittle a spoon from a stick or someone take apart a musical instrument to clean it and then put it back together again. The movements are often rhythmic and repetitive; there is skill shown in the detail and satisfaction is gained from thorough completion of the task.

I remember very clearly, as a child, sitting for at least an hour watching my dad build a wall in our garden. He was very methodical – moving repetitively and mixing the mortar and carefully scraping it onto the bricks one at a time. I sat in the sunshine and enjoyed every minute, watching the wall come into fruition. I also used to love to watch my mum hang out the washing, carefully straightening all the clothes onto each line until the airer was full and the clothes were blowing in the breeze. As a mother I understand how unusual it is for children to sit still for so long but now I know I was in an ASMR state, watching them and enjoying every second.

Personal attention

Similar to touch triggers, personal attention ASMR triggers feature someone taking care of you in some way, providing comfort and prompting a sense of love and security. Often these routines involve some level of personal care, maybe giving a facial or styling hair, giving a treatment or an examination.

Very often the actual purpose of the treatment is secondary to the naturally occurring triggers within it. An example would be someone attending a reiki treatment and being triggered by the practitioner arranging a blanket over them, walking closely around them and carefully placing their hands on or very near the receiver. Or perhaps having a facial cleansing treatment where the beauty therapist is paying close attention to your skin and being gentle and soothing. It is not the clean skin or thought of it that is the trigger, it is all the actions, sounds and care given during the session.

Another notable trigger here is that the therapist is not making eye contact or trying to connect with you, but working *on* or around you. The feeling of being cared for without perhaps the social anxiety of being looked at too deeply as an individual is comforting, and you are able to enjoy the triggers made around your body freely.

Personal attention triggers are popular in video form. In the same way the in-person triggers are delivered, so is the session in video form received. Common examples are videos where the ASMRtist appears to be putting make-up on you, giving you a medical check-up or an ear examination, or measuring you for clothing, or cutting and styling your hair. A well-liked video concept is 'Tucking you into bed', as it involves lots of different sound triggers, close-up movements, clothing movements and vocal triggers. These are often given the title of 'role play' videos, where of course the creator is giving care in a typical 'role' such as the beautician or medical practitioner.

Taking personal attention to a deeper level *would* involve eye contact. This is mainly a trigger in video form as it seems to be the most comfortable way to receive it: 'I see you, I accept you and I love you' is something I believe we should all repeat to ourselves in the mirror. This can be difficult – most of us, if not all, have our insecurities. Taking action and running the risk of being 'seen' by others can require a lot of courage for many, so allowing yourself to receive eye contact in a completely non-judgmental situation through video form can be amazing practice. Perhaps this is the first step to being able to do this in the mirror, then finding more self-acceptance and being able to follow your heart in action, even in a small way. It isn't always necessary to do big things, little ones can be just as powerful. From small ripples come big waves.

Empathy

Empathy plays a role in ASMR in three distinct ways, and tapping into our empathic responses can enhance the ASMR experience greatly.

The first, and I find this very rarely discussed, is when we are triggered by empathising with someone. Some of the strongest ASMR responses I have had in my life are while sitting with a friend, drinking tea and listening to them tell me a story of something that has happened to them. The moment when I begin to empathise with their situation I can feel intense tingles, almost as if in that moment we are connected. I become calm and centred and am able to tap into a suitable response for the situation, and others who have had the same experiences have explained a similar response.

The other more obvious empathy trigger is watching someone else receive a treatment of some kind, connecting with how that feels for them and receiving almost a secondary treatment for yourself. In video form this might be watching someone receive a massage. Your empathy responses, coupled with the sounds and voice in this situation, can increase your experience greatly. Similarly, for those who don't particularly feel the tingly sensation but have strong empathic responses, these videos can be a perfect fit.

The final empathic trigger is another connection response – as you feel an empathic connection with the person delivering your triggers. As we all have our preferred stimuli, we can also have our preferred practitioner. Take something as simple as tapping, for instance. Tapping may be our favourite trigger of all time, but the person who delivers the tapping can determine our experience of it. A person we feel no connection with might produce no tingles at all from their tapping, whereas feeling comfortable with someone can make all the difference and completely enhance the experience.

'Empathy has no script. There is no right way or wrong way to do it. It's simply listening, holding space, without judgment, emotionally connecting and communicating that incredibly healing message "you are not alone".'

Brené Brown

UNINTENTIONAL ASMR

Unintentional ASMR is the most popular form of attention-induced trigger. Before the first whisper video arrived on YouTube many people would watch videos that were full of ASMR triggers even though the creator didn't intend it that way. They were just recorded in a close-up, soft fashion, creating lots of sounds from their demonstration and talking fairly intimately into their mic along the way. To this day, videos appear on YouTube all the time filmed in this way. The comments below them come from many ASMR viewers and the creator must wonder what on earth is going on. 'Mister Rogers', Bob Ross, shopping channels, cooking demonstrations and nature programmes, along with the thousands of YouTube demonstrations, can all be classed as unintentional ASMR triggers. My favourite unintentional ASMR video of all time, and very popular with the community, is a video of Bjork. She is taking a TV apart and talking about how the inside looks like a little city. It is also very insightful – her mind is beautiful.

There are a huge number of potential stimuli then, and equally so many different ways to deliver them, especially in video form. The many different types and styles of ASMR videos can greatly affect the experience. As discussed earlier, there are re-enactments (role plays), which are very popular and can be made with a combination of triggers. There are 'no face hands only' videos, or videos with just sound such as whispering and no visuals, or hanging out together chatting or rambling, quietly delivered tutorials like 'how to make a salad' and show and tell videos, which are usually based around close-up visuals of showing and talking about a personal collection of items. There is most definitely something for everyone.

There are also different *ways* of recording an ASMR video using a variety of sound and visual equipment: the sound can be recorded in stereo so that it appears 'ear to ear' for the listener. Alternatively there is 'binaural' sound, which is similar to stereo only it is recorded even more realistically, as if in the same room. The microphone 'hears' more like a human head and picks up the full spatial aspects. There is also 'mono', which is sound-recorded in just one channel and would be heard at an equal constant level in both ears, and 'omnidirectional', which is sound-recorded equally from all directions around the microphone. Any camera can be used, even a smartphone, and in fact lower-quality visuals and/or audio can sometimes enhance the experience as they give a more intimate, less produced and personal feel. Natural lighting can add a cosy ambience, as if inviting the viewer into your home during the day for tea, whereas the use of more high-tech lighting and perhaps incorporating colour can create more immersive visuals.

WHAT IS ASMR IMMUNITY?

Along the journey of discovering ASMR we hear of something called ASMR immunity. The name is a little misleading; it should really be called something like 'ASMR over-stimulation', though that's not quite as catchy. For those who experience the ASMR sensation and have been experiencing it all their lives, it might just come along unexpectedly or for a fairly short space of time. Upon discovering ASMR videos on YouTube the feeling is available at the touch of a button, whenever and wherever you would like it and for however long you would like. It can also, for some, be felt more intensely through video form. This means that people are suddenly feeling it more intensely than ever before, more often and sometimes in places they have never felt it before. It's like an overload of tingles. This happened to me and it was mind-blowing and all through my body all at once at times. However, after a while the body tends to balance out and calms this down for you. Your reaction becomes less intense and sometimes goes away. The general advice here is to take a few weeks, or a month or two, away from videos. Once you come back, you're ready to go again. From my own experience the sensation has never disappeared, just become less intense and at times faint. However, I have never lost an intense feeling from working with in-person triggers. Some report that they just need to find a new trigger that works and the tingles will come back, but from my experience a break from videos now and then is always good if you can.

Childhood themes

I believe the stimuli that resemble childhood memories trigger an emotional response as well as a tingle response. Those that resemble nurturing actions, sounds and visuals from nature are for me the most effective to trigger the tingly sensation and the intense relaxation that comes along with it. These are soft and caring and make us feel comfortable and therefore safe.

For those who don't experience the tingles, the emotional response from triggers that positively stimulate memories from childhood or nature still provide deeper relaxation and immersion, so they can be effective for more people and can be used on a regular basis to engender comfort and safety.

Childhood memories are most often recalled by ASMR experiencers when attempting to explain the sensation to others. I have many myself, and am often sent stories by friends in the community who watch my channel. One writer's memorable early experiences were of the local librarian tapping her nails on the desk, and also when she peered over the bank counter to watch the cashier counting out bank notes. She told me that she saw the 'essence of ASMR as completely pure and innocent' and what she saw in my videos and others were 'nurturing and hark back to blissful childhood memories and experiences'.

I vividly remember asking my brother and sister to trace letters or pictures on my back as a child. The game would be to guess what they were drawing and I would pretend not to know so that the tracing would go on for longer. Many people recall having their feet carefully measured in the shoe shop when about to start a new school year, or playing the game 'Round and round the garden' on the palm of the hand. I also loved it when an adult would straighten my coat when I was little – pulling out the sleeves of my jumper, folding down my collar and straightening me out. The sound of the fabric, the talking quietly to me and being close up, plus the feel of the movement around me, was a magical combination.

TRIGGERING A CHEMICAL RESPONSE

It is very possible that ASMR triggers create a chemical response in our bodies, that our responses to them are causing our bodies to generate beneficial chemicals. We know that deep relaxation in general lowers the release of stress chemicals and encourages the parasympathetic nervous system to become active (the 'rest and digest' part of the nervous system). Therefore it is very possible that if deep relaxation is achieved through ASMR triggers then we could be lowering the release of stress hormones like cortisol and adrenaline and encouraging the release of beneficial hormones. The most obvious chemical would be oxytocin, which is often called the 'cuddle hormone' as it is released through social bonding like cuddling, stroking a cat and breastfeeding. This could be released with triggers such as personal attention, for instance. Serotonin is known as the 'happiness hormone', and among other things regulates mood and sleep, while endorphins – often associated with exercise – are linked to the reduction of anxiety and pain. It is possible that one or several beneficial chemicals are released during the ASMR experience and I hope that through further research we will learn more about our chemical response specifically through the ASMR experience.

How to find your ASMR triggers

As I've mentioned, ASMR often seems to occur in the more sensitive of us, the empathic or perhaps introverted. These are people who are more likely to experience daily life with a heightened sense of awareness of everything around them. So, to find your ASMR triggers, start by asking yourself if you have ever considered yourself to be a sensitive person. If so, then what are you sensitive to? It could be something as simple as smells, bright lights or lots of sounds at once. Alternatively it could be something a little more complex – like being affected by other's moods, absorbing the energy of a group of people when you walk into a room or feeling inner or physical pain more than others seem to. Or do you often find yourself overwhelmed when you have a lot to do, or become emotionally invested in a film to the extent you feel almost in it? Perhaps you sense things about people without even speaking with them, picking up signals from their body language, what they *don't* say when they speak and a general atmosphere.

Next I suggest thinking about examples of times as a child when you may have felt comforted, dreamy or absorbed in a situation. Did you ever ask others to stroke your hair or whisper in your ear when you were little, and how did it make you feel? Did you enjoy watching people do things and become absorbed in their task? What examples in this chapter jump out at you as something you remember from your own childhood?

Now consider your current life. Starting with where you are right now while reading this, ask yourself if there is anything in your environment around you that you find particularly comforting. Perhaps it is something you are wearing, or have you been inadvertently comforting yourself while you read – playing with your hair, fiddling with a piece of jewellery or feeling the edges of the book's pages?

Think about your daily life. What is it you find comforting? Is there anything in your work or school environment you tend to focus on when you become tired or overwhelmed? What places do you retreat to and recharge? What is it about those things that brings comfort to you? Is it a sound or a texture perhaps?

Sometimes it can be very hard to know what we find comfort in as we become older. Our lives can be so loud, busy, full of responsibility and mental noise that it is very difficult to note the intricacies of ourselves through our daily experience. This is why childhood experiences, or at least those from times when you had less responsibility and fewer things to think about, can be helpful. If you can remember any examples from younger years, you can probably deduce what it was about those memories that was comforting for you. Did you feel anything physically from them? If so, what was it? Did you feel positively in terms of emotion? And what emotion was it? Did they make you feel transfixed, dreamy or sleepy? What parts of the experience made you feel that way? Think back to the types of triggers – sounds, visual, touch, personal attention – to help you.

All of these prompts are a way to help you find triggers you would be drawn to now. If you are able to come to a conclusion about what those experiences entailed and what it was from the experience that made you feel that way then, using the categories in this chapter, you will have some idea of how to seek them out again. This will lead you on a journey to finding your own most effective ASMR triggers.

TRIGGER TESTING

For those who don't remember anything in particular and would like to start from scratch on their ASMR journey, here is a way for you to dive into the wonderful world of triggers.

Choose three triggers from the sound and touch trigger examples that resonate most with you from those discussed in this chapter. Some easy options would be a piece of crinkly plastic like a wrapper, a book and a small bowl of dried rice or something similar to represent sound. For the touch triggers, a large make-up brush, a pen with the lid on or just your fingers are good starting points.

1. As well as you are able to, find a quiet and calm place to sit. Take a little time to breathe and be in the moment. Take three long, slow breaths in and out. Concentrate on your breath as you draw it in and allow it to leave. Notice where you are sitting and feel yourself secure and relaxed in your position. Take more deep breaths if you need to. The important thing is to feel as relaxed as you are able in this moment and do not feel rushed to do this exercise. Take as much time as you can.

2. Choose one of the sound triggers and very slowly and carefully make sounds with it – 'play it'. Create as soft a sound as you can manage, nice and slowly, taking your time. Watch and listen carefully as you go. And as you do this notice how it makes you feel, visualise in your mind all the aspects of that object. Take your time and enjoy the moment.

3. Next, take one of the touch triggers, the pen for example. Use the pen with the lid on to draw shapes on your forearm moving down to the palm of your hand. If your hand is quite ticklish then just stay on your forearm. Up and down, round and round in circles. Feel the pen gliding over the

surface of your skin. Notice how it
makes you feel and in your mind follow the pen
around and trace the pattern with your eyes.
Slowly enjoy the moment.

4. Do this exercise with all of the triggers you have
    chosen, taking the time with each one to notice
    how it makes you feel. Is there a sound you
    liked the most? Did you enjoy any of the touch
    triggers? These could be your triggers.

5. You can then, if you wish, go online to search for
    those triggers and see what you might feel from
    them through video form with any of the creators.
    Watching videos while wearing headphones can
    mean you hear the sounds more intensely and
    that the triggers feel closer and more intimate.
    Start at a low volume, then increase the sound till
    you feel comfortable. Remember to notice how
    everything makes you feel.

Finding your own triggers and being in control of your
own sensations is a powerful tool in self-learning. Not
only do we become more aware of our sensory perceptions, but each time we experience a trigger and take the
time to notice how we feel, as a result we look within
and become more present in the moment. Whatever your
ASMR sensitivity, this is a practice in mindfulness and
a gateway to regularly using relaxation and meditative
techniques.

These can help you to be calm more often, feel less anxious and sleep better, among many other benefits. ASMR is so much more than a feeling and throughout the rest of this book I will show you how to learn the techniques, gain a deeper understanding of them and be able to use them in your daily life.

Chapter 4

Healing Principles and ASMR

Once we learn what ASMR actually is on a physical level and how it affects us we can then explore how it fits into our daily lives and how it can be useful for us. Here I will look at common issues like stress and anxiety, and how sleep, a big issue for many people, contributes to our health. I will also draw on information and learnings from other complementary therapies and mindfulness techniques and explore how ASMR links with these concepts, so that when we put ASMR techniques into action we're able to gain a greater understanding of how they are influencing us. Many of these concepts and therapies can be described in some way as healing.

Stress and anxiety

Stress isn't entirely our enemy. Some level of stress is important for us as human beings. We have evolved through the fight or flight response, and need an amount of 'good' stress to motivate us and to help our self-development. We experience a level of stress when we watch a horror movie or ride a rollercoaster, and we are also in stress mode when we have a job interview or need to stay alert during our working day. It's our body's way of helping us to complete those tasks to the best of our ability, but it is also the fastest way to disconnect with our body and inner world.

By considering how much stress we have experienced in a day, we can ensure we give ourselves proper rest. It's part of being kind to yourself. We must listen to our body.

There are many different types and levels of anxiety, which often follow a build-up of stress, long periods of chronic stress or stressful events. In our body this is a release of stress hormones like cortisol and adrenaline, prompted by worry, fear or nervousness. Anxiety can occur out of the blue, or it can be in response to the processing of or reaction to a past event.

Some of us live in a near-constant state of anxiety and it becomes our normal state of being. This is called chronic stress. I lived that way during my experience of PTSD. My mind was so busy re-living a past trauma and worrying about current events and future events that may or may not come. This caused a cycle of constant stress that just added to the issues. Through this there was no space to concentrate on how my body was feeling, so my mind and body were disconnected. Life was an ongoing state of living without control of mind and therefore body. Through specialised cognitive behavioural therapy, exercises and patience I was able to work through these issues and find balance.

For general levels of daily stress, and for maintenance purposes, once I learned about cortisol release specifically, it helped me to visualise this release as an image in my mind. When I felt the wave of anxiety appear I would visualise it lowering and a light appearing in its place, leaving space for a feeling of stillness or joy. It has been proven that through visualisation and belief we are not only able to change the way we feel and what we take in through our sensory environment, we can actually create positive change on a cellular level.

'The moment you change your perception is the moment you rewrite the chemistry of your body.'

Bruce H. Lipton

In the short term, for general 'useful' amounts of stress, the immune system is boosted for a while to keep us healthy while we complete the task at hand. However, prolonged periods of stress with increased levels of cortisol inhibit proper function of the immune system. Imagine that your body is sending most of its energy to keep you safe under stress – it doesn't have enough to keep the rest of your functions working at full capacity. Your digestive system, organs and immune system are all secondary to your body dealing with the stress.

You can see how easily this can create a cycle of health issues. Again, we must listen to our body. Be kind to ourselves and use proper self-care, as prevention is much easier than cure. It's also more fun.

It can be useful to understand what type of personality we are as well, so that we can prevent over-stimulation. Pushing ourselves to try new things and controlled exposure to some things we find a challenge is good for us, no doubt about it. But understanding when we need a break is important – there is no shame whatsoever in saying no when all your friends want to go out for the third weekend in a row!

What is healing?

I have often been reluctant to use the word healing in my work with ASMR. I communicate with so many people from all backgrounds in all different countries and it has become clear to me that the word 'healing' – and even more so the word 'healer' – has many different connotations attached that don't necessarily reflect what it actually is intended to mean. But it is notable how many people choose to use the word themselves when talking about their experience with ASMR.

Healing very simply means the process of regaining health. However, if we have the understanding that our health does not just include our physical body, it also means the process of gaining optimum health in body, mind and self or spirit. We can then understand that to heal is an ongoing process of growth, self-understanding, acceptance and self-love.

A healer is someone who facilitates that process. To be a healer is not to have the ability to miraculously cure someone using supernatural powers, it is the ability to feel compassion, love and empathy towards others to the point where you are able to aid them in their healing journey and connect with their natural, inbuilt healing ability. Ultimately the healing process is undertaken by the receiver and this is the understanding of both parties. The ability of the practitioner to connect with the receiver, and the acceptance of the receiver to be responsible for their own healing, is very important, in ASMR healing as in any other context.

So this means that 'making you tea' healing can be just as effective as other healing techniques if it is performed with the correct intention by someone with compassion and love. And the person receiving the 'tea' finds what they need for their own personal healing journey from that. A healer helps to provide the space for healing to take place, which means we all have the potential to be healers in one way or another.

Complementary Therapies and Fundamental Principles

From studying sound therapy, aside from learning about the power and practical applications of sound and understanding sensation further, the most important things I learned were about taking on greater responsibility for my life choices and about connecting more deeply with my true self, from the awareness of intuition to the principles of grounding, resonance and entrainment. They were important lessons for me personally and I found them very applicable to my daily life and my approach to ASMR. I would like to share these with you.

What is mindfulness and why is it so important?

Mindfulness is the practice of being fully present in the moment and working to quieten down the overactive mind. Often our body is in one place, completing a task, and our mind can be focused on something completely different, not noticing what the body is doing. This is not healthy for us, especially if our mind is busy re-living an event from the past or worrying about what might happen in the future. Our body can be working on the task and experiencing the sensations of it and while our mind is busy worrying, our body is also absorbing the sensations of that anxiety and stress.

Living life in this constant state of disconnection with the present can be overwhelming, tiring and very stressful. I see it as being in a constant state of trying to do many jobs at once. Merge that in with juggling general stresses and strains through a busy day, making endless decisions, trying to maintain relationships with others, and we're in terrible trouble. Living life in this way each day results in us missing out on so much of what the present has to offer us. It creates a cycle of behaviour where we are not enjoying life to the full and it prevents us from making healthy decisions to move away from this cycle of stress. It also has an effect on those around us and can cause the same issues for them.

To live mindfully is not to completely reject or judge the chatter in our minds, but to observe it, accept it, sit with the experience of it and, once we recognise it does not serve us, let it go. In practice, it is becoming aware of where we are and what we are doing, taking in our environment through our body and noticing how we feel. There are many ways to do this, from the simple noticing of our breath to movement techniques and the use of sound. Whichever way works for you is always the right one. For myself, ASMR and being in nature are my two main mindfulness practices. I incorporate the act of being present in whatever I am doing throughout the day as much as I can, using ASMR techniques, self-observation and deep breathing.

Incorporating mindfulness into our lives, beginning with the simple concept that we can observe our own mind and the physical reactions to it, is one of the most important things we can learn as human beings. Along with good nutrition, water and exercise it is the best preventative medicine. We know that stress is the cause of great dis-ease within the body. I remember my nanna saying, 'Calm down, you'll make yourself ill' – I had no idea of the full extent of what that meant when I was little. I do now.

The power of intention and positive affirmation

Intention is the place from which our actions come. Two people can have the same tools at their disposal and yet the outcomes from the use of those tools can be completely different if their intentions are different. The outcomes can have positive or negative effects, for both parties involved.

Imagine you are faced with the task of brushing the hair of a loved one and you have two minutes to do it. If you are rushed or annoyed at having to do the task, you may do it with a little extra force, perhaps tugging and causing pain. If you are excited to go and do something else then you are likely to do it very quickly, missing sections along the way. However, if your intention is for this to be a relaxing experience for your loved one and a mindful or connecting experience for you, then the style of your brushing will be more careful. In each scenario the same two minutes are filled with different intentions and therefore actions. The latter produces very different and far more positive outcomes for both parties.

Similarly, when we find ourselves in a position to help others our actions may come from a personal 'need' to do so. This can lead to a counterproductive outcome, where we can perhaps 'act' too much and not really help at all, but rather enable. If we come to see our role as a 'facilitator' then we can act in a way to help others to be stronger for themselves. The outcome here is again beneficial for both parties.

This may at first seem quite strange to talk about in conjunction with ASMR. However, intention is vitally important. For a content creator, correct intention helps carry out the role of caregiver in a more efficient way. For the receiver of the content it helps to you to decide what you intend to use it for and then be clear *how* you will use it. For those giving in-person ASMR sessions, it is important to understand that how you are feeling at the time and what your intentions are will come through in the treatment you are giving. As a receiver, if you know what you want or need from the treatment you are more likely to experience it.

'You need to have a word with yourself!' This saying would make me giggle when I was little. When in my adulthood I learned about mindfulness it came back to me and made me smile again. There is so much wisdom in a lot of the old sayings we heard as children. I'm not even sure if the people saying them really knew the depth of them at times, they are just habit. There are also those sayings we would never say again now we know what they actually mean – language is powerful; be careful how you use it.

Positive affirmation is really important in ASMR; we use it a lot in video content. Sometimes we need to hear acceptance of ourselves through the voice of another, repeatedly, before we can begin to naturally think it on our own. 'You are beautiful, you are kind, you are enough.'

The most important language we use is to ourselves because it's ultimately how we feel about ourselves that determines how we behave and communicate with others. Then, if you imagine your behaviour can be mirrored back to you, perhaps even through synchronisation, then what you give you can receive ten-fold.

'The world as we have created it is a process of our thinking. It cannot be changed without changing our thinking.'

Albert Einstein

Training ourselves to speak positively both internally and outwardly is a matter of deliberate action that takes will and practice. Accepting that you have a right to live in peace in yourself, and externally in harmony with our planet and all other beings, is the first step. We are all hard on ourselves at times, but what we are born with is what we have to work with. Whatever conditioning and beliefs we have been raised with, good and bad, may not serve us as we grow into the world. We can take responsibility and choose who we would like to 'be' and this begins by repetitive affirming thoughts and behaviours. Whatever you think and do, you invite more of into your life by affirming it. So affirm good thoughts and good actions and reactions. Be kind to yourself. Both in action and in thought.

SMILING AFFIRMATIONS

We don't just smile because we're happy, we're happy because we smile. The simple action of forming a smile shape with the muscles on your face sends a signal to your brain, which it then interprets as happiness. If your brain is then telling you again that you are happy, you smile more. Smile at yourself in the mirror and it has double the benefit – you have someone beautiful smiling back at you!

Intuition

Intuition – your 'inner knowing' – is having inner wisdom about something without the use of conscious thought.

This can be when we allow creativity to flow, or times when we do not allow thoughts and reasoning to come in and inhibit our actions, when we know how another person is feeling without the use of speech or thought, or that moment of knowing the right decision before rational thought creeps in to tell you why it might not be such a good idea, or be too risky, or too difficult. A very simple example of this would be if you meet someone and know 'deep down' that something is wrong and you want to ask. This is a natural intuitive response. However, conscious thought can then come in to tell us why we shouldn't say something. If we follow our mind here we are inhibited in this moment. By side-stepping our thoughts and telling the person anyway, we would be following our initial knowing or intuition.

In the practice of mindfulness we intuitively use all of our senses to experience the world around us, occupying ourselves with all the textures, smells, sensations and colours of nature to become present in the moment. The more regularly present we are, the more we are able to notice our intuition. The same process happens in ASMR – intuitively responding to the triggers using our senses leaves less space for conceptual thinking.

'All true artists, whether they know it or not, create from a place of no-mind, from inner stillness.'

Eckhart Tolle

Grounding

'Bringing ourselves back to earth' is important in our daily lives. It's a very simple concept and something that once we become aware of we might realise we knew all along. Think of the times when you are running around and busy or stressed out and erratic; you may feel light-headed or have a slight headache and that all your energy is gathered at the top of your body. When you are relaxed and still and having a calm day, you will feel 'heavier' and more likely to be aware of your feet being firmly on the ground. Grounding is when you rebalance your energy. A method of doing this, which I found to be useful not only practically but also through the visualisation of it, is simply being aware of your contact with the ground below your feet and being in the here and now. You can even use your deepest voice to tone or hum a deep vibrating sound.

There is also 'Earthing', which is the term used for grounding when you take off your shoes and walk barefoot on soil, sand or grass. Connecting your body with the Earth's surface electrons, even for just 30 minutes each day, can have proven health benefits. In terms of my ASMR experience, and keeping myself calm enough to work, I do this during the day and before I film my videos to help me focus and become present. I also 'ground' myself through visualisation as part of my night-time ASMR routine.

Self-protection and boundaries

An ASMRtist is largely a caregiver and I know many of you reading this are caregivers too. Self-protection is crucial and it's something I learned that really helped me. In your ASMR experience, as a complement to your daily practice, it could help you too.

In sound healing and other therapies we talk about self-protection in terms of our energy field merging with another person's and the need to separate ourselves after treatment in order to keep our own energy flowing and positive. Absorbing energy from many clients can cause burnout for the practitioner. I like to explain this in another way for those who may not think in terms of energy fields – it is about being conscious of not taking on responsibility for someone else's journey, learning or healing process. As I have explained, understanding your role as a facilitator means you are able to disconnect yourself from the empathic connection you have with another so that it doesn't continue for an unhealthy length of time, and so to be responsible and in control of your empathy. Then we can use it when it is needed and not allow it to take us over. This is part of establishing boundaries with others so that you can aid them in learning and coming to decisions on their own and not be used up to the point where you are exhausted and need help yourself. If we imagine ourselves as batteries that need to be recharged, that can help in terms of using our energy wisely.

Resonance and entrainment

This is something I specifically learned in sound healing. People often tell me they begin to feel calm and sleepy around me, and I know that many of you reading this will have had the same experience from others. Learning about resonance and entrainment gave me a greater understanding of this process.

Sound healing is largely based on the principle that everything in the universe has its own resonant frequency, a frequency of vibration or sound determined by its size, shape or thickness. This then means that everything in our body – every organ, bone, every cell – has its own resonant frequency. The body is seen then as a culmination of sounds, like an orchestra, and when the body is in 'dis-ease' it is out of tune.

Entrainment is when one strong vibration causes another less powerful vibration to meet itself, synchronising together, like matching the footsteps of someone you are walking besides or arriving at the same breathing rate as theirs. The subject of entrainment is quite vast and covers synchronisation through sound, visuals and touch stimuli. I would suggest further research if this is something you are interested in. However, for the purpose of this section and as my takeaway in terms of my ASMR practice, I quickly came to see how our presence and how we behave can cause another to behave in the same way. When we cuddle a crying child not only are we comforting them and increasing oxytocin levels, our steady breathing is causing them to calm down and resonate or synchronise with us. In the same way, being calm and quiet around another, either in person or through a video, can cause them to slowly become calm and quiet in your company. On the other hand it is very difficult to have a screaming argument with someone who is not shouting back. As they say, your vibe attracts your tribe.

THE IMPORTANCE OF SLEEP

It is very difficult to fall asleep with a busy mind and if we do it is likely we will be restless through the night or have vivid dreams, affecting our sleep quality. During the most stressful periods of my life I can remember waking up in the morning feeling as though I hadn't slept at all, no matter how much sleep I'd had.

There is an abundance of information available to us to explain how sleep is important for our brain health, metabolism, mood, memory function, immune system and much more, not to mention that lack of sleep puts us at greater risk of various serious conditions. So it is vital that we do everything possible to keep ourselves healthy during the day to achieve the best-quality sleep we can. Sometimes simply being aware of the importance of our sleep can act as a reminder to make sure we allow ourselves enough time for it.

Switch your thinking to see your sleep window as an enjoyable experience, something to look forward to. Even if you do not fall asleep straight away and with ease, at least you are allowing yourself that time of rest. Preparing for sleep can be a fun and a mindful experience, itself a self-care practice and time for you to unwind from the day. Knowing that this time is important for your general wellbeing and health means that you are more likely to do it for yourself, especially if you have responsibilities to perform during the day. Taking care of your wellbeing means you can perform these to the best of your ability.

This doesn't relate so much to those who have extreme insomnia or other chronic sleep disorders, perhaps due to medication or medical conditions. Those of us living in near-constant physical pain are very often awake with it and my heart constantly goes out to those people I hear from, many through my videos, who struggle in this way. You are all true warriors.

The power of the senses

Through our senses we are inextricably linked to the world around us. To be in touch with our senses is to be present in our body, aware of our surroundings and, with practice, in control of how these can affect us. All sensory stimulation in our environment has the potential to cause us to feel something, be it via our hearing, sense of smell, touch, taste, sight or mind. We feel negative or positive responses from these, often without even noticing what is happening. For example, when we experience a distressing noise that impedes our ability to think or concentrate, or when the sight of something makes us feel stressed or tense. What we allow into our environment via the use of technology is often thought of as negative, but it can also be food for the mind. And even if we are bound or obliged to be surrounded by some things that have a negative effect on us, through awareness we are more equipped to deal with and understand or prevent any negative effects.

ASMR in practice causes us to be aware of all of the subtleties in our environment by helping us to become more in touch with our senses. Once we gain this deeper understanding of ASMR and how it combines with our lives we can see how every moment can be an enhanced experience. With this knowledge we can also learn to apply filters and make decisions according to what is healing or beneficial for us and what isn't. We can use what we know to be positive to improve every aspect of our lives – to take responsibility for ourselves and how we feel, learn self-care, heal from within and project a healthy spirit outwards.

The power of the voice

Our voice is the instrument we are born with. It carries energy in its sounds and language, meaning that no matter how you feel, and how you might try to disguise it, your emotions come through in your voice. It's there in the tone, pitch and speed with which we speak and many other signs we're not even aware of. Next time you listen to a podcast or audiobook, try to tell when the speaker feels happy or is smiling, and when they're less happy or sad. Listen to how the emotion is conveyed – even if the speaker is speaking in another language. With practice and awareness, you can tell by the sound and delivery of the voice what emotion they are trying to portray (or disguise).

Try listening to the conversation on a table near to you when you're next out having a drink or meal – even without looking at facial and body language you should be able to learn a lot about the relationships involved. This isn't to say that everyone listening would be able to understand this language, but with practice you can understand the power of the voice to show feelings.

During my time as an ASMRtist there have been many instances when I have recorded videos after a busy, sometimes stressful day – being a mother, part of a busy family, a homemaker, with all the usual ups and downs that brings. (Sometimes I feel I would barely make any videos if I only recorded them on 'perfect' days.) When I record a video that doesn't show my face at all – a very simple scenario where I am making tapping sounds with an object and quietly talking about it all the way through – the video is relaxing and I very much enjoy my time making it, as the speed is slow and the delivery is very calm and peaceful. The comments below the video are always full of kindness and love from a very special community of people, but there will be two or three comments asking if I am OK. 'You seem a little tired,' they will say. I know they can tell from the minute change in my voice that I am tired after a long day and perhaps have underlying stress about something. The emotions we communicate through our voice can indeed be very subtle. The awareness of the importance of our voice in connecting with others leads us to understand that what is inside, so without: that what we project from inside us, no matter how subtle, has an effect on others. This is why self-care is extremely important, not just for ourselves but for others too.

The power of sound

We also know that certain types of music create different moods. The music we listen to for going for a run would be completely different to the music we would play for relaxing after a long day. When we need to feel energetic we play something upbeat and when we need to calm down we play something soothing. Perhaps after a break-up we need to hear songs in a minor key with lyrics about lost love so we can sit in that mood and process our feelings. Sometimes we might use music and sounds of the opposite mood to change the energetic state we are in.

Other sounds work in the same way. We know that the sound of a pneumatic drill outside our workplace can have an effect on our mood, just like a colleague repeatedly rapping their finger on the desk. These sounds can cause anxiety, agitation or feelings of stress, whereas a babbling brook and birds tweeting gently while we have a leisurely walk can cause us to feel calm and content.

Sound can also bring about emotionally charged memories from our past. For instance, a regular commenter and friend on my channel, Jennifer, remembers very clearly when she would spend time at her grandma's house as a teenager. She always felt safe with her grandmother, who lived on a lake. She would listen to the sounds of the waves lapping on the shore. These sounds now conjure up fond memories for her of feeling relaxed and safe.

In ASMR, sound is extremely important because not only can it communicate a mood, it can also create feelings of calm, trigger pleasant memories linked with nurturing and produce a physical sensation and state of relaxation that potentially sets off a positive chemical reaction. If sound can cause us to create feelings of safety and intense feelings of relaxation then it can be used in a conscious way for the reduction of anxiety, depression, pain, for better sleep, and more.

Instruments of sensation

Sound healing instruments frequently used are the voice, Himalayan (Tibetan) singing bowls, crystal singing bowls, tuning forks, gongs, drums and the didgeridoo, among others. These instruments are not usually listed as ASMR triggers, though it is certainly possible to make triggers with them. After all, they are also objects and practically any object can be used in ASMR. I have incorporated my sound healing instruments in some videos and learning about how these instruments are used in healing can help us to understand how other sounds work and can help us.

An interesting introduction to sound healing would be attending a sound bath. Don't worry, it's fully clothed! These are groups of people lying comfortably around on the floor covered in blankets with their head on a pillow and listening to the beautiful sounds coming from an instrument. It can be a gong bath, a crystal bowl bath or a mixture of instruments. I like to attend a sound bath with minimal instruments and prefer not to mix metal with crystal. I find metal instruments to be a stronger, more 'clearing' experience and the crystal bowls gentle and soothing. As the instruments play around us we physically feel the vibrations through our body, the sound through all our senses. We are bathed in sound waves. If we are able to surrender to the process we can travel from our usual waking and functioning beta brain waves to alpha and theta. Alpha means to be awake and relaxed. Theta is a very deep state of relaxation, close to being asleep, where we can be inspired or process memories. Many feelings can come up in this state during a sound healing session or sound bath, which is why it might be called a clearing process.

When we sing or play a Himalayan bowl we hear the fundamental tone of that bowl, but there are other notes apparent at the same time, called harmonics. As our brain is busy processing all the notes playing, our mind empties and we become still. This is why bowls are used in meditation, and why sometimes a bell or cymbal is used beforehand. The sound gains our attention and focus.

Buddhist monks use the voice in chanting. If we replace the busy mind chatter with a repeated word or phrase we again become still and focused. If those words or sounds, for instance the sound Om or Aum, are toned using the tongue to create a deep chamber in the mouth, we can hear harmonics in the sound. A vibration is also created, which in conjunction with the harmonics keeps us in a focused and calm state.

Through learning about how instruments are used in meditation and sound healing applications, we can have a greater understanding of how listening to a simple repetitive sound – like tapping on a mug, for instance – can lead us to a state of focus, 'mind-emptiness' and then relaxation.

'When you get in touch [through the six sense organs] with an image, a sound, a smell, a taste, a touch, or a thought, your mind receives that signal and immediately goes through material stored in the subconscious, searching for any connection to the sensory input.'

Thich Nhat Hanh, *Peace Is Every Breath*

The power of touch

Touch is also a language, and the very first we learn. As children we are reassured, soothed and guided. We learn connection, discipline and more, all through our sense of touch. From birth we communicate through receptors in our skin that connect to our nervous system. In fact, touch is vital to our development as babies. We know that if babies are not held enough they do not thrive, and that skin-to-skin contact has a range of benefits post-birth. We also know that a simple touch from a loved one can relieve pain. We use a gentle touch to communicate our empathy and understanding and through this touch we can show our willingness to share the burden of a problem. We touch others to show our congratulations too. Touch is clearly a very important tool in our connection with one another.

Without even realising it, touch is also often used for self-soothing – when you place your face in your hands, a hand over the heart or rub your earlobe. Many of us do these things without realising they are actually self-soothing actions. Basically we are innately wired for communication via touch and becoming aware of that helps us to use touch techniques when we might need them.

In a study in 2006, named 'Touch Communicates Distinct Emotions', researchers found that emotions such as anger, fear, disgust, love, gratitude and sympathy can all be communicated through touch. For the practical use of ASMR this is crucial so that, when we consider touch triggers on ourselves and others, we understand that we can influence the experience by our feelings at the time – enhancing the experience in a positive way if we are calm and loving. Not only do we need to move softly and slowly with our actions in order to achieve the ASMR experience, but also take steps to ensure our intentions are to communicate positive emotions through our touch.

The ability to connect or disconnect with the world around us is essential. Being responsible for ourselves, self-care and balance in all things are vital for our well-being, for our healing journey and how well we live. Both with ourselves and with others.

ASMR in practice is a holistic approach for self-healing and healing others. It incorporates the importance of sensing everything around us, observing ourselves, mindfulness, connection to and taking care of our body, recognising the value in ourselves and others, positive affirmation, using intuition, self-love and care. Above all, it helps us to feel connected and at peace.

Chapter 5

Your New 'ASMR' World

Awakening to the world of ASMR is a gradual process. We seem to do so in stages, and at each we become a little more at peace until suddenly the world is so much bigger and more colourful, and everything and everyone in it more beautiful. It's a healing journey all of its own.

In this chapter we're going to work through the three stages of awakening your ASMR sensitivity together. I will explain what they are and, later, what we can learn from them.

I notice often that people seem to go through the same things when learning about ASMR, in line with my own ASMR journey. I love to read all the comments from people experiencing it at different levels or stages. It's fun to see comments from people who have just found out about it. I'm really excited for them and it reminds me of how I felt when I first discovered ASMR. They can range from 'wtf am I watching?' to an in-depth analysis of minute 6:03 when I tapped on an object in a certain way while looking at the camera and happened to make a specific mouth sound. The contrast between the two perceptions gives me joy.

Stage 1: Discovery, letting go and the 'art of noticing'

No matter how we discover ASMR, it can feel very weird at first and lots of people have this as a first reaction. So let's be honest and begin with that. You may have heard about it from a friend, seen it on social media, read about it in the press, watched your favourite YouTubers try it out or, like me, stumbled across the term ASMR while searching for something to help you sleep. It is good if you've discovered it in a way that helps you to understand its effects quite quickly, but if not that's OK. The fact is you found it and I am happy you did.

> 'The easiest way to get into a meditative state is to begin by listening.'
>
> Alan Watts

If you come across a video it's usually someone making a sound with a random object, whispering into a microphone from close up, slowly waving their hands up to the camera lens looking serious and dreamy or pretending to be a doctor of some sort. Some of these images we might, up until now, have only seen in advertising or presented in a sexual way.

ROLE PLAY ASMR

I briefly explained 'role play' videos earlier but didn't go into too much detail. Let's do that now. This term has connotations attached to it, so it's not my favourite, to be honest, though its origins are very innocent and it is exactly that – playing a role. We do it in kindergarten, nursery or pre-school.

Role play videos are wonderful. I absolutely love the immersive aspect of them and the personal attention. They are a relaxing performance of daily life situations where the ASMR experience can occur – popular themes are having a haircut, a doctor's appointment, a visit to the make-up counter or an eye test. There are so many. All of these situations involve direct (eye contact) or indirect (around or on you) attention, quiet sounds, soft speaking or whispering and slow actions. They are the perfect way to combine multiple ASMR triggers and present them in one long, relaxing and varied session. However, showing them to a friend, partner or family member as a stand-alone representation of ASMR cannot always be sufficient explanation.

In October 2018 I worked on an immersive live event with a brand. It was the first time I was able to lay out all the different triggers and ways of presenting and experiencing ASMR in one event. There were videos playing everywhere, including various role plays, with places to sit and watch them with headphones, but also a hands-on spa, items to feel and make sounds with and a tactile area for textures. It was a multi-sensory exhibition.

I found that so many people were able to take their partners along in order to explain what ASMR feels like to them. Rather than a video, which might not give the full impression, there was something in that event for everyone to relate to and gain further understanding.

I believe we all have an innate understanding of the concept of ASMR and that it isn't very different from so many things that are naturally incorporated into our lives already because they help us to feel good. We just need an explanation that makes sense for us as individuals.

Once we accept it, let go of initial impressions or judgements and take a deeper look into ASMR, the feeling takes over and we notice different things. At first we might have focused on the person 'doing' the ASMR – what they were wearing, their make-up perhaps or accent; the things that we tend to notice about anyone that we meet. All the surface things, you could say. We might notice their actions and feel they are a little alien to us. Once we begin to feel something physically, we can't let go of those initial perceptions. We focus on that instead and what may be causing it. I remember the exact moment this happened to me; it was such a shift from one perception to another. As soon as the physical feeling came over me, suddenly everything made sense – all the looks at the camera, the mouth sounds, the actions on the objects, the physical movements. Everything was done to make me feel this sensation. It happens just the same with people who don't necessarily feel a blanket of tingles, but who have the same realisation through whatever positive feeling they experience. Feeling relaxed because of these simple actions makes everything clear, and we feel thankful to the person doing it to help us to feel that way.

'I'm tapping on things everywhere I go!'

This is probably the reaction I see the most. Suddenly everything around you has a sound, a texture and details you may not have noticed before. I call this learning the 'art of noticing'. You become a details person, or if you were already you're more aware of it now. It's really fun to begin looking at things around you – in your home, on your daily commute or just as you walk down the street – that have been in position for such a long time that you forget to see them any more.

You might notice how things are messy and want to straighten them up. You might even imagine yourself making your own video or giving an ASMR session. What things in your house would you pick out for their ASMR qualities? What is it you notice about them?

The supermarket is a fabulous place for noticing; you find yourself tapping on all the things you pick up before putting them in your basket – crinkling the bags and feeling the texture of the fruits and vegetables. Then you might notice the sounds you make yourself with your own body – listen to your own breathing, the mouth sounds you make; hear yourself as you swallow your food and listen to the sound on your skin as you scratch an itch, for example. The sounds you hear in a video are accentuated because the ASMRtist's microphones are usually turned up high, but if you listen closely you can often hear these subtle sounds from yourself.

Now you are starting to reconnect with your body and your surroundings. Already you are living less in your mind and more through your body and senses. This is similar to the way you experienced the world as a child, before the complications of adult life took over. Watch a small child when they are out and about – see how they stop to examine or play with the smallest things like a leaf on the ground, to feel different surfaces and textures, to put their hands into water or mud at every opportunity. They are naturally drawn to experience the world through their senses and intuition, and their inhibitions are not yet developed. Learning to observe the world again is very familiar to you and feels free and fun.

Stage 2: Making the connection: familiarity, warmth and your inner child

Now you are more aware of your self and your surroundings, it is common to start remembering times from your past when you felt the same familiar sense of comfort. Some of these experiences will stand out to you so much that you can still remember every detail now, even if you haven't thought of them in such a long time. It's common to remember negative events from our past more often so it's an uplifting feeling to begin to recall more and more positive moments. It's affirming the positive, you could say, as you remember feelings of safety and what it was about a place or situation that made you feel that way, or thinking of nurturing times with a carer and how lovely those comforting actions were.

On examining our sensitivities in this way, we connect on a deeper level with our childhood. Ask yourself what kind of child you were. Do you remember trying to explain these sensations to anyone? What happened? Do you remember feeling ASMR at all? What made you happy? What made you sad? What part of that child is the same now? Do you still perhaps need the nurturing, comfort and safety you felt back then? Even if it is just a moment here and there. Do you feel safe in your daily life more often than not? If not, then what do you need to change? Feeling safe is an important part of being less anxious and able to fully rest and be present.

Not all of us are lucky enough to have had nurturing experiences when we were younger, and this process might be a time when we can start to understand how and when we needed them. How has this affected who you are and how you behave now? Do you bring any of these actions into your relationships now? Is there anything you can do for yourself now to heal that? It could be a painful experience to examine all this, of course, but it's a step further towards emotional freedom and the hard work pays off.

So many emails I receive from viewers through my time online contain stories of not feeling sufficiently nurtured as children, be it through abuse, neglect or simply parents not understanding our needs as sensitive people, especially in difficult times when parents were working or struggling with their own issues.

Connecting with your inner child by experiencing the world in this new sensory way is a healing process. You are connecting with who you were and your past experiences and incorporating them into your current awareness, perhaps fulfilling the side of you that was suppressed by the need to 'grow up' or 'be good' or learn responsibility quickly.

Now is a good time to pick up a game you used to love to play, or do an activity or hobby that you enjoyed as a child. Go on! Whether it's jumping in puddles, playing Twister or relearning how to roller-skate, it's fun to be lighthearted and allow yourself to feel the world. Part of being a successful adult is knowing when to let go, allow creativity to flow, be 'childish' and not be afraid of judgement from others.

TALKING TO YOUR YOUNGER SELF

Try talking to your inner child – your childlike self – by affirming kind words to that part of you. You could start your sentences with:
'I remember ...',
'I hear you ...',
'Thank you for ...',
or 'Well done for ...'.
You can be the person you needed as a child, and re-parent yourself.

Healing the inner child and 'gaps' in our childhood is another way the role play videos work for us. They either re-create situations we remember fondly as children or re-create the attention we didn't get as children. Not to say they 'regress' us at all, but they allow us to experience now what we might have missed out on then. They can also create a feeling of nostalgia, bringing back times of joy, contentment and relaxation. They even turn some negative experiences into positive. Perhaps you didn't enjoy going to the dentist or flying. Watching a relaxing version of a dentist appointment or a flight attendant taking care of you can affirm the positive and balance out any negative memories you may have, or the sense of vulnerability that you felt as a child.

Deeper connection

Not only are you reconnecting with the world around you, here and now, you are also reconnecting with your-self. The 'art of noticing' works within as well as without. When we become used to noticing our physical reactions to ASMR, it is common to begin to notice more of our physical and emotional reactions to other things – how we feel when we encounter different situations, both good and bad. It might be our reactions when people talk to us in a certain way, how we feel when we consume different types of media, eat different types of foods or respond around different types of people.

You are developing a deeper sense of awareness and connection, not just with your outer world but with your inner world too – a heightened sense of awareness and connection to how you feel, when you feel and what those feelings might be. This supports us in our ability to make healthy decisions for ourselves and prompts us to take action to invite more of what makes us feel good into our lives.

This brings the emergence of a new awareness, a 'sensual awareness'. It is the path to living a more heart-led intuitive life rather than just mind-led, achieving greater balance and ultimately connecting with your intuition. When we act more from a place of how we feel than how we think, we invite more joy into our lives, we smile more, feel more confident, care less about other people's judgements. If we allow our mind to judge us first, we're practically asking for others to do the same, as if we are attracting negativity towards us. Many call this 'raising your vibration' and bringing more compassion into the world.

Listen to your body and use your mind as a tool. Not the other way around.

Stage 3: Integration: a useful tool and a shift in consciousness

So many of us can't find complete silence to sit in quiet. Some of us can't find any quiet at all if we live with other people and have busy lives and responsibilities. ASMR sounds, similarly to sound healing instruments, are a transition or alternative to being alone in meditation. A gradual, gentle washing away and distraction from the mental noise, slowly bringing us to peace. It can be very scary to flip the switch, even if you know where it is, and sit alone with yourself. Thoughts come up and feelings with them, and there is no distraction to drown them out.

An ASMR video in headphones can be the nearest thing to true quiet that some of us have experienced in a long time. But it can also be a much more comfortable form of quiet. Complete silence sitting in meditation is an uncomfortable concept for many of us. We are so accustomed to living in a high level of physical and mental activity, around loud noise and often in our fight or flight stress mode, that it's near impossible to stop. Imagine being on a treadmill for a long time and then when you get off your legs are all wobbly and you can't stand straight. Moving into ASMR awareness is a similar adjustment – we have to work through a process to get to a 'normal' walking pace again.

Through regular connection with our new ASMR world, through awareness, understanding and repetition, the benefits start to become clear. Perhaps we begin to make time for and enjoy more relaxation moments. Through remembering nurturing actions from our past we can ask others to care for us in the same way, or we remember to do it more for our children, relatives or friends. We might incorporate self-soothing actions into our daily lives, noticing things we instinctively did before and doing them more.

This is the process of recognising how ASMR can become a useful tool for us. As we notice greater detail in ourselves and the objects we are surrounded with, we see more beauty in others and have more compassion, both in people and in animals, in nature and the environment, and we feel more integrated with the world.

We realise that not only can ASMR be useful for us, it affects those we spend our lives around too. 'Perhaps I can incorporate my new awareness into how I care for others. From my new, more rested perspective, I can pass on my wisdom to others. I'm not so afraid of being seen so much any more, I feel more powerful and calm'.

What these stages also teach us

Growing into the world of ASMR is in part the 'unlearning' of some of the conditioning of our lives so far, through the media we consume, our communities, schooling and friendship groups. We of course gain huge positives from our learning and most of us are extremely fortunate for what simply our place of birth grants us, but there are also inevitably ideas and concepts we might unknowingly accept as truth. And the world of ASMR can challenge these for us. Here are five learnings I want to share:

Intimacy

Firstly ASMR reminds or teaches us that there are lots of different types of intimacy, such as compassion, kindness and empathy, and they are separate from sexual intimacy. These different connections are all part of the ASMR experience. For example, a person onscreen moving close to the camera, giving eye contact, moving slowly and providing a stimulation of senses doesn't necessarily mean sexual stimulation. These particular types of intimacy can be fulfilling emotionally and beneficial for our overall wellbeing, helping us form more natural and fulfilling relationships.

It's OK to be sensitive

In fact it's a very valuable part of who you are. You have an ability to process deeply and listen to intuition. You are more likely to be creative and imaginative in everything you do. You are able to understand those around you at a deeper level and be more compassionate, and are good at making others feel comfortable because you understand the subtleties in their environment. You think situations through before acting and make more sensible decisions for yourself and others. Of course, as we have established, sensitive people are able to sense and be more connected with their environment and, with their developed sense of empathy, make it a better place for everyone. They are very valuable members of society.

We don't need more 'stuff'

The material possessions we already have are valuable. Most of us are aware by now that trying to achieve true happiness through possessions, money, food – through consuming – is not ultimately fulfilling, but putting this into practice in today's world, where the accumulation of material things and money is congratulated at every turn, can be hard. ASMR gives us a gentle lesson in loving, being grateful and seeing the beauty in what we have. At this point I have to say that for me, being an ASMRtist, this is a problem because due to the nature of my videos

I find myself with a massive collection of objects and instruments that sound good, not to mention my crystal collection. I need to listen to my own advice! At least I realise I don't need them, right? When I see Marie Kondo advise us to give thanks and appreciation to items we possess and clothing we pass on, it makes me smile. I see that we gain this same perspective through ASMR.

'I only have one suit, that's all I can wear.'

Al Jolson

You're not as alone as you first thought

Feeling a little different from others can sometimes cause a level of social anxiety – the fear of being 'seen' or being out in social situations. I would go so far as to say that just being in this world can cause that. Life can be so tough. Realising there are other people who feel the same way as you do, and being part of a community, is very empowering and gives us confidence to get out and be ourselves more. Suddenly 'different' doesn't mean strange as so many would lead us to believe. It's just a difference in perception.

We are connected to each other

ASMR is a wonderful way to discover that we are all linked in ways we might not have previously expected or experienced. When I read the comments under videos it becomes clear that we all need to be loved, nurtured and told we are good enough and that we are doing well – no matter who we are, what our age, skill or intelligence, or where we are from. Ultimately, we are all our inner child, 'the true essence of who we are', going through life learning, experiencing and growing. We all have struggles and are doing our best with what we have. Not one person is 'better' than you; they may be further along in their journey than you, but that's a gift. We can learn from and be inspired by those people. Also not everything is as it first seems. Don't judge a book by its cover, as they say. Sometimes people behave in a way that looks as though they have everything completely sorted in life but underneath they are struggling like crazy to keep up the act or image. Be compassionate with those people, they really need that. Be careful who you follow and choose your idols wisely. Some of the greatest heroes in our world don't have a large following on social media. In fact they don't have time to be on it; they're too busy saving lives.

Ultimately we are all reaching towards the same thing. Love, acceptance and belonging.

Chapter 6

Make ASMR Sensitivity Your Superpower

n this chapter I am going to show how, using every-thing we have discussed so far, we can incorporate ASMR principles and techniques into our daily lives in order to effect change. By looking at *how* ASMR is cur-rently utilised by so many all over the world and for *what benefits*, we can learn how to use our enhanced sensitiv-ity to improve our lives and the lives of those around us, to ultimately become more focused, self-loving, calmer, confident, conscious and mindful individuals.

ASMR really does change lives. Just the simple dis-covery of the name has for so many connected the dots, by giving an explanation to something that might have been a mystery to them since they were a child. Then there are those who discover not only the name, but how it can help to improve a current health or well-being situation. There are also so many people who have never known the tingly sensation but have found a whole number of benefits for themselves through ASMR. We are in the midst of a mindfulness and self-development revolution and ASMR is proving to be a valuable part of that.

Before we look at the common uses of ASMR, here are some of the basic techniques so that when I refer to them later you will be able to pick out your favourites and try them for yourself. This list is always expanding and changing. Sometimes as an ASMRtist, even after all these years of practice, I might intuitively do something different in a video and not even realise until it is pointed out in the comment section. If you have any favourites or have invented something new, then let me know on social media or below a video on my channel.

ASMR on yourself

Always move gently, slowly and being careful to mindfully breathe at the same time. You could pinch and release tiny sections of hair, run nails up and down the inner forearm, trace circles on the palm of the hand, or run nails or pads of fingers along the back of the hand. Take a pencil and trace around your hand lightly on a piece of paper, or use light touches around your face, lightly tap your nails on your face, or find an item you know would feel nice, like a large make-up brush, and run it across your cheeks. Use a head massaging tool across your scalp or lightly brush your hair. Similarly, use any item that would feel nice on the skin and try the same movements with that; it is good to change up textures and sensations.

ASMR on someone else

As a receiver you should always be mindful of breathing and letting go of tension; as the giver, be slow and gentle. Remember, the lightest touches can be just as powerful as, if not more so than, harder or more deliberate contact. Always set the intention that you are there to aid the receiver in their relaxation process and help them to receive it as best they can according to however they feel at the time.

Using your fingers, either with the soft pads or the nails, trace letters or patterns on the receiver's back. This can be on bare skin or through clothes. Tools can also be used on the back, like a comb or a brush. Try running a string of beads across the back, or a bunch of fresh lavender. Use your imagination to find what you think would feel soft and gentle. The same tools can be used on the arms and shoulders.

Hair play and hair-brushing, when done lightly, carefully and slowly, is very effective. Use different tools on the hair, like wide-toothed combs, fingers and massagers.

While applying the hands-on techniques, talk gently or whisper to the person. It doesn't need to be about an important subject, just use the power of the sound of your soft voice. You can talk about what you are doing, describe the session and use positive affirmations, such as 'You have beautiful skin', 'It is very relaxing to give you this treatment', or 'I am enjoying this time together'.

Try a session of sounds around the body. Discuss what sounds you both enjoy and 'play' them softly around the person, paying particular attention to the softness around the head. If you would like to be super-creative why not re-create your favourite role play video.

To provide an ASMR session for another person can be a valuable experience for both parties. Always check what the person is comfortable with, what they would like you to do and for how long. Make sure you have a cosy setting, and it also helps to have a drink of water to hand as it is common to feel thirsty after a relaxation session.

'You cannot truly listen to anyone and do anything else at the same time.'

M. Scott Peck

ASMR videos

All ASMR video content is labelled as to what triggers it features and some are labelled according to intended use also – for instance 'for sleep', 'for anxiety' or 'for study'. Others can be more general or contain a combination of triggers. It is for you to decide which videos contain the combination that works best for you. It could be the sounds that are used, the colours, the 'feel' in terms of the type of setting in which the video was recorded. It could also be the specific creator who works for you personally. The trick is to find a creator with whom you feel a connection and then try out lots of different content, noticing how each makes you feel. You may not even be able to figure out at first exactly why some feel better than others. It will be helpful, eventually, to be able to pinpoint your positives about a video so that you can look out for others that are similar.

You could even set up separate playlists of videos to use for different things. 'My favourite videos for study', 'for sleep', etc. It is also helpful to use a variety of creators, styles and triggers so that you can change up your viewing and keep your reactions to the videos fresh.

Headphones or not?

The preference again is yours, and sometimes it depends on the creator or the type of video, the way it was recorded or what you are using it for. If you are having a relaxing moment to yourself, then sitting with headphones on could provide an extra sense of privacy for you and block out the sound from your environment. Perhaps if you are studying then having a video playing quietly from a speaker in the room will provide suitable background sound.

Enjoying a video with headphones makes the sound far more intense and means you are able to hear all aspects of not only the subject of the video, but also the details of the voice or object. If you listen over a speaker on your device or with a lower-quality speaker you may hear less detail in the background and more 'top-end' frequencies in the recording. This can give a more unintelligible feel to the content. It really is about your personal preferences, and my suggestion would be always to start with a creator you bond with, pick out videos that you are drawn to and then listen to them in different ways – with or without different types of headphones, different speakers and at different volumes. You can even try combining two or more videos at once. If you have a favourite creator you enjoy for their voice and another who is great with sounds, then play them both at the same time, on your computer or multiple devices.

Part of the fun of using ASMR videos is that there are so many different ways to watch and listen to them, using all types of devices and different sound equipment. No way is better than another as they all produce a different effect. Some of the best ASMR videos ever recorded use a smartphone with the inbuilt microphone. Mostly it's about the creator, their voice, the sounds they use and how they deliver all those things and, ultimately, if they make you feel comfortable.

BODY SCANNING

As you use ASMR techniques on yourself, or receive them from another, try a mental body scanning or body sensing exercise before you start.

It's very common to be holding tension somewhere in our body without realising. Perhaps during a meeting or watching TV, suddenly your awareness comes to your body and you realise you are clenching a fist or your leg muscles are not relaxed. This is a sign that you are not fully present in your body and your attention is in your mind, or simply that you are not relaxing as much as you are able. If you are taking the time out for relaxation, it would be even better if you could experience the full benefit.

While being aware of your breathing in and out, scan your body. Bring your awareness to your feet. Imagine each toe relaxing and that relaxation moving up through each foot. Then loosen the muscles up your legs. Let go and feel them sink down into their positions. Then follow your mind up through to your chest. Visualise and feel all your muscles relaxing with each breath you take in and out. Relax your shoulders and let go of tension all the way down your hands until you reach the tip of each finger. With each breath in and out, release all the muscles in your body as you work your way right to the top of your head.

To finish, always tell yourself something positive: 'I am relaxed', 'I am totally at peace', 'I am beautiful', 'I am just how I am supposed to be', 'I am enough'.

Sleep techniques and practises

'Falling asleep, staying asleep, and going back to sleep when awakened require an ability to soothe oneself, to feel safe in the world.'

Elaine N. Aron, *The Highly Sensitive Person*

ASMR is most commonly helpful for the purpose of sleep, whether we're suffering from insomnia or have general trouble falling asleep at night. It seems that our biggest issue is being able to achieve a clear mind and adequate state of relaxation, enough to be able to fall asleep, and ASMR really helps with this.

Firstly, it provides us with the beginnings of a bedtime routine or ritual. Then it clears the space to become calm before laying down our head, giving something for us to focus our minds on and a sense of close connection with a person who has dedicated their time for us in that moment. If that person is speaking and moving slowly it also sets a sonorous rhythm with which we can synchronise ourselves. Then, through the use of our chosen triggers, we are able to feel the tingly sensation and/or the deep sense of relaxation that comes. Our brainwave state changes, along with physiological changes, as we move into a relaxation state, and our natural sleep processes can operate.

We're more likely to achieve a restful night's sleep if the mind is clearer beforehand, and there is less chance of waking up due to restlessness or unsettling dreams. Our mind is more rested, as well as our body, and our natural regenerative body functions take over. During deep sleep our bodies release hormones to repair and rebuild tissue, and cortisol levels lower. The sympathetic nervous system, controlling our fight and flight response, has a chance to finally take time out. Our immune system also has space to function fully.

Once we are able to achieve a more full and restful night's sleep we are set up to be less stressed in the daytime. This will have a huge impact on our daily lives – we are able to be present enough to make clear decisions and be more thoughtful in our actions. It is possible to be patient and understanding with those around us and aware in their company. Everything we do throughout our day and night is connected. Better sleep helps us to break a cycle of negativity and create a new, more positive one.

There are numerous ways to utilise ASMR before going to sleep, or if you are woken or naturally wake up in the night. People use videos, sound-only downloads and self-soothing techniques (or if you have a partner, sibling or friend kind enough to give you an ASMR session, that's lovely).

GADGETS AT NIGHT

At night the pineal gland releases melatonin in the body, which is a required hormone for inducing sleep. Blue light emitted from screens has been found to have negative effects on melatonin production, but warmer colours like yellow and red light, which have a higher wavelength, have been found not to do this. Consider a blue light filter for your device, or switching it on to night mode later in the day; you can also turn down the brightness. Be mindful of how much screen time you are having in the evening.

Videos or sound-only streaming and downloads

Video content is currently most prevalent on YouTube; however, you can find many artists with content available for download or streaming on other services. There are several ways to watch a video before sleep, so consider what works best for you, especially if you share a room or a bed with a partner.

Some of us are very susceptible to relaxing when we watch ASMR videos and only need to watch or listen for a few minutes, others will need longer. Depending on which position you sleep in, you could try headphones designed for sleeping. You may prefer to listen without headphones if you like the sound that comes out of the inbuilt speaker on your device. You can even try a combination. Sit up in bed watching your favourite video wearing your headphones and, once you are relaxed and ready to lie down, take out the headphones, lay your device face down and fall asleep to the sounds you hear as background noise, or use headphones with your eyes closed, perhaps lying down.

Using a speaker in the room and playing the sound through that is a really good tip if using ASMR to help your child sleep. To have a speaker in the room with no device to hand takes away the temptation to pick it up and keeps their eyes away from a screen. Snuggle time in front of a video together beforehand can be lovely, but once they are tucked up with the lights off, the sound can play gently in the background to send them off into a deep sleep.

MY FAVOURITE ASMR SLEEP ROUTINE

For me, I like to have a video playing on my device in the room while I prepare for bed. You can use the inbuilt speaker on your device for this or connect to an external speaker; I have a mini Bluetooth speaker I use sometimes.

I occasionally look at it while getting ready. This gives me the sense of having the company of a relaxing and positive person with me as I prepare for sleep. I feel myself slowing down to their pace and being more mindful in my actions. Then I watch the video in bed for a while till I feel sleepy and relaxed. Finally, I lay the device down, snuggle up and fall asleep to the 'top-end' high frequencies in the voice and sounds from the video.

Self-soothing techniques

Using ASMR techniques on yourself can work very well to achieve enough relaxation to get to sleep. You can be your own therapist by becoming mindful of your actions as you get yourself ready for bed. Draw your awareness to your movements in every step of your routine, listen to the sounds as you brush your teeth and place the toothbrush back into position (see Moments 7 and 8 in Chapter 8).

Before settling down for sleep, perhaps try some of the self-soothing techniques such as stroking the insides of your arms and watching as your fingertips make an impression on your skin. Tap gently around your face while drawing awareness to your breathing. All the time, listen to the sounds as you move. If you feel able, then this can be done in front of a mirror. Giving eye contact to yourself is a lovely way to bring yourself back to 'you', the essence of who you are, at the close of day. Always give yourself a smile if you can.

It is known that a cooler body is able to fall asleep more easily, so using an ASMR technique involving a hand fan or electric fan can work two-fold. Many people feel soothed by the sound of a fan in the room as it is a form of white noise and feeling the air move across your face, listening to the sound and lowering your temperature all work together to help you fall asleep.

Most of us can picture the romantic vision of a woman spending time at her dressing table at night – removing make-up and taking a long time to brush out her hair – something that we might have seen in old films. Become your own Forties film star by spending time brushing your hair gently in front of the mirror, counting the brush strokes and listening to the sound of the brush as it passes through your hair close to your ears. If you have less or no hair, then a simple head massage with an oil would be a lovely alternative. The idea is that you are spending time caring for yourself in a present and mindful way, always drawing attention to your breathing, using slow deliberate actions and listening to the sounds.

With someone else

An ASMR 'treatment' from another person is a wonderful way to fall asleep. Not all of us are so lucky as to have someone with us who is able to help, but for those who are I would suggest taking full advantage! You can joyfully repay the care another time.

This could take the form of a relaxing session in another room before heading off to bed, or while lying in bed ready to drift off. Most of us are familiar with comforting techniques that are used on children to fall asleep, lovely nurturing actions that perhaps our family or carers used to do for us such as stroking the hair, whispering gently, or running fingers up and down the back and across the arms. All of this can be done on another person regardless of their age. As we get older we do not lose the ability to be soothed by these actions, which tells me we still need them at times. If you feel comfortable enough to ask for something like this, then do so. Most of us like to be needed and if we don't vocalise and explain what we want and need from others we're not always likely to get it.

THE 4–7–8 BREATHING TECHNIQUE

This is a technique I regularly use in conjunction with ASMR. It works particularly well after an especially busy day, or if I have been very late to bed and need to bypass my usual routine. It is promoted by Dr Andrew Weil and is based on ancient yogic traditions. The tip of the tongue is held behind the teeth on the roof of the mouth throughout. Inhale through the nose quietly and count to 4, hold and count to 7, then breathe out to a count of 8. On the exhale, making a louder 'whooshing' sound with the mouth. If you would like to know more, there are videos online by Dr Weil showing how this is done.

The second most common use for ASMR is stress and anxiety. From general levels of everyday stress to anxiety attacks, regular ASMR will help you to gain focus, positive affirmation and distraction from a stressful situation, and of course feel relaxation. If you are struggling with general stress or severe anxiety issues, do talk to your doctor and ask for medical help. ASMR techniques, mindfulness practices and exercises can work very well in conjunction with any help you may need from your medical practitioner.

How to use ASMR for stress

Of course there are many types of stress and you should try different calming techniques according to your personal situation. For general stress reduction or prevention, ASMR can be used at any time of the day as and when required, although I would not recommend playing an ASMR download in your car when driving or operating machinery at work! If you're walking or taking public transport to work, though, this is a great time to listen. It helps you to be present and focused before your work activity begins. At times when you are not able to change a stressful situation you might be dealing with or to act on a worry, using an ASMR video or download to occupy your mind when you don't need or want to be thinking is very useful.

Being able to recognise when you need a break during stressful times is an important self-care practice in itself. Even if you are not able to do anything about it in that moment, at least you are listening to your body and recognising your feelings. If you are able, take a short walk outside, listening to your favourite trigger with a set of earphones. This will help you to have a change of scenery, take in some air and feel calm from the sound. For that time, you can block out any external sounds and gain a fresh perspective on your environment, which will help you feel more grounded and calmer.

You could also try just the self-soothing techniques on your own. Take yourself away for a moment, sit in quiet if you can and choose something you know to work for you, for instance tapping your fingers around your face. Focus on your breathing. You could pick up a small object and make soft sounds with it, run your fingers over the surface and feel the texture. You could listen to an ASMR trigger you like while doing this. All of these actions will bring your awareness to your senses and away from your mind or physical feelings of stress.

Watching a video will give you something to focus on, either with headphones or without. Engage with the ASMR sensation you feel. If you are particularly stressed, always notice your breathing at the same time as this will be extra help for you to be in your body as well as focus your mind.

For anxiety or panic attacks, depending on the severity I would suggest using a downloaded video file either on its own or combined with your personal attention/self-soothing techniques. If you are able to have someone do them to you that is great, but on your own works too. You can be your own comforter just as effectively as you would comfort another person.

FOR ANXIETY AND PANIC

Choose a video from a creator you feel especially connected to and safe with, someone who uses a lot of caring eye contact and slow movement. While watching the video, focus on long slow deep breathing as much as possible. If you have fast or erratic breathing at first, just keep going with the intention to become in control and to slow it down.

Know that you are having a panic attack. The fight or flight mechanism of your nervous system is working for you at this time. Acknowledge that this is a natural function of your body, but it is just not needed at the moment. Tell yourself that you are OK and you are going to be calm soon.

If you have your hands free, then use simple movement to soothe yourself, stroking actions along the arms or thighs perhaps – whatever feels right for you at that time.

Follow the eye contact, slow movements and steady breathing of the creator, keeping your breathing deep and slow. 'Reframe' the situation to a positive one in your mind. 'My nervous system is working hard for me. Soon I will be calm again. I am OK.'

Keep breathing and focusing on it till the rhythm becomes slower. Keep breathing and keep focusing until you are calm.

Brain breaks

Many of us use ASMR videos not just for sleep at night but also during the day and earlier evening, to enjoy a moment of general relaxation and meditation. If you are in a loud office or busy public area this might be a welcome break for you. Even just five to ten minutes to take a brain break can make a positive difference. Taking time out in the daytime for relaxation and meditation not only reduces stress and anxiety and helps us feel happier, it will also increase productivity by lengthening the attention span and increasing memory.

For self-ASMR techniques during the day, keep a head massager with you. Those with the many slim metal fingers are wonderful for inducing tingles and relaxation when you would like a quick dose. Bend it open to widen the tongs and glide it slowly across your scalp. You can close your eyes at the same time and of course focus your breathing if you like. Take as long as you can. If you have someone to do this for you, it's a bonus.

ASMR AT WORK

Keep a large clean make-up brush in your pen pot and brush your face with it as you read an email. For me, I find that it helps to have another focus while I read and it prevents me from becoming overly emotionally invested in the content of it. I am more able to stay balanced enough to reply thoughtfully and objectively.

Study and focus

For sessions of work or study that require long-term focus there is a lot of content online dedicated to sounds only, with or without barely-there use of voice such as unintelligible whispering or muttering. These are typically longer videos containing a simple mixture of sounds, either made one at a time or layered over each other. The concept is to have sound playing in the background that provides a slow and even backdrop, with little interruption or change-up of rhythm. From my experience this works best played over a speaker in the room, but others may like to use headphones, especially if there are other people in the same space or nearby making sounds, which could be a distraction. Using ASMR in this way seems to keep us in a steady state of focus so we can complete the task in hand.

This is similar to using white noise for the same reason or to fall asleep to. White noise is described as many frequencies at once, all at the same volume and intensity. It is usually quite high-pitched, whereas 'pink noise' is also many frequencies but at a lower pitch. The idea is that this sound will override any outside sounds and again provide a steady backdrop without sudden changes in rhythm or pitch. You can use an ASMR soundscape in this way that is more detailed and to your personal preference. It is always a good idea to listen around, explore and find a good fit for you.

TINNITUS

Some people who struggle with tinnitus have found specific ASMR trigger sounds can provide relief for them. Playing just the right trigger sound seems to lower the intensity of the tinnitus frequency by masking or cancelling it out. We have no research evidence for this but I have been told about it by several sufferers.

Other benefits

There are so many other specific uses for ASMR that it would be impossible to cover them all; people use ASMR for lots of different reasons. Here are some of the more common uses that I am aware of, and particularly that I have sufficient feedback on to be noted. If there is something in your life that you feel ASMR could support you with, I would suggest reading through the ideas in this book to find those that resonate with you.

Stressful event/performance

ASMR is a wonderful preparation tool before a stressful event, such as exams, a nerve-wracking social situation, interview or meeting, or before public speaking. These are situations where a little 'good stress' will help give you some adrenaline to improve your performance; however, your fight or flight response is not so helpful and can prevent you from performing adequately. ASMR can also be used after these events to wind down, either in video form, with self-soothing techniques or both.

Pregnancy and labour

So many people tell me how they've used ASMR throughout pregnancy and during labour, particularly in labour when lots of eye contact and a soft motherly voice are very supportive. I would suggest again choosing a creator with whom you feel a close connection, perhaps even one with their own children as you'll know they have been through the same as you, and watching a long video including lots of positive affirmation, soft flowing sounds and a caring steady voice throughout.

Loss

Losing a loved one is a stressful event with so many different responses and processes involved. Use the power of ASMR for company, positive affirmation and as something to focus your pain onto and to receive comfort in return. You can imagine you have told the ASMRtist your story and are receiving a kind response.

Receiving the kindness of a stranger with no specific reason attached can be very freeing and easy – when you have lost a loved one there may be lots of sympathy surrounding you, but usually that is coupled with talking about the situation and pressure on you to respond in a particular way (or even try to make the other person feel better). Sometimes you just need kindness without any conditions attached. Ultimately it is a healthy distraction and a chance to do some self-healing in private.

Pain

ASMR is very often used to help cope with physical pain. This could very well be working on a physiological level if we consider what the experience of the tingly sensation might be and which hormones are possibly produced during relaxation. We can at least safely assume that it is a distraction from some types of pain and a chance to refocus the mind on something else.

LONELINESS

This is a major issue in our communities these days; we have bigger populations than ever, yet more lonely people. Perhaps it is indicative of our time and being so busy and living more in our own minds. ASMR has become a part of everyday life for many people who use it to have company when needed. Even if that person is not physically in the room it can be comforting to have a soft-spoken voice nearby.

If you regularly watch a creator who is caring and speaks 'kindly', it can be a huge positive for you when you do not experience others speaking to you that way in your day-to-day life. Many people you come across in your day may not have the time to do this. An ASMR video can be used in the background while completing household tasks in the same way that the radio or a podcast can; it's just a more relaxing and slow version.

Confidence and positivity

ASMR is a natural confidence booster. Positive and affirming videos can combat social anxiety and positively affect how we feel about ourselves. The creator has devoted their time to you and they care about your wellbeing. Similarly, someone applying the techniques on you is good for your positive self-image. Knowing that they want to spend their time with you is a lovely feeling.

The positive action directed at you is a form of belief training that you are valuable and loved. Having an inner knowing that you are these things means you are more likely to attract love and kindness in your day-to-day life. You are also more inclined to work on your self-development, perhaps by having the confidence to learn new skills, try new activities and make new friends.

One of the most wonderful things about ASMR is that there is something for everyone. There are so many triggers and ways to deliver them and this is constantly growing. You may even invent your own. Through the process of discovering what works for you, you are also going through a process of self-learning and listening to your body. Through giving and receiving in-person treatments you are becoming more connected with your loved ones and you have a way to nurture each other when needed. Even the existence of the term 'ASMR' and everything that surrounds it means you have more of a reason to ask your partner, friends and family to do things for you that are helpful for your wellbeing. It isn't just something you know 'you like'; you know how it can be life-changing for you.

'Everyone shines, given the right lighting.'

Susan Cain, *Quiet*

Become a healer with just a cup of tea in your hand

You have at this point gained a deeper understanding; how does your cup of tea appear to you now? You have the power to transform a simple task and/or a simple object into a healing experience for you or someone else. By being present at every step of your actions and by using each of your senses, you can add mindfulness practice to the smallest and perhaps previously meaningless parts of your life. Through using ASMR techniques you have the power to change your life, beginning with your morning cup of tea.

PART 2

Your Guided ASMR Moments

Chapter 7

How to Use ASMR as a Daily Practice

N ow you are an ASMR expert! You have all the knowledge you need to take on the techniques as a daily practice. So how about I help you to do that with some simple steps? Who knows how just a few little thoughts and actions throughout your day could not only impact your life, but also the lives of those around you? This section is about how to become your own ASMR guru.

Whether you are a seasoned ASMR experiencer or this book has been your introduction, all of the exercises in this chapter will help to develop and deepen your sensitivity. These are guided examples of how ASMR can bring change to your life, helping you to live more in the present and relieve anxiety and stress. Repetition and little mental reminders are the key to life-improving practices; the more we walk the same path of behaviour, the deeper it gets. We create neural pathways in our brain through repetitive responses and actions, and over time these responses and actions become habit. Equally, if you have current negative habits, then you can imagine how the brain pathways are well-established. New pathways can be developed by taking on fresh challenges and deliberate repetitive practice. The more you do something, the easier it becomes and the sooner it becomes habit.

One of the advantages of ASMR is that it requires no extra necessary items or accessories, only what you already have in your life and all of the content you might want to access is free. Similarly, the steps I have devised are easy to do and allow you to develop your awareness at your own pace, on your own and without any pressure.

My intention is for you to understand how to find and use your ASMR sensitivity within the everyday, and in doing so be open to all of the sensations and benefits it has to offer. ASMR has always existed in daily life 'offline', but now we are lucky enough to have so many more options via the internet. Recently, though, for some, ASMR appears as something that only exists through video form, especially those discovering it for the first time. I believe the internet is a tool to bring us all together, to spread knowledge and create further human connection all over the world, and through these steps I would like to demonstrate further how we can integrate the techniques both online and in person, and how the two methods can happily complement each other.

JOURNALLING

If you are someone who loves to journal, feel free to begin a new notebook for your ASMR writings. You could perhaps make notes on how each step makes you feel. When you discover any of your preferred triggers, record how each one affects you, which provoke a stronger response and those that may be less effective for you. As you repeat the exercises, look back at previous notes to see how your responses may have changed. This could be a fun way to document your journey, help your awareness become a regular habit and learn to develop your 'noticing' practice.

Before we head into the guided steps, let me pause to tell you a short story; something that, after all these years of living the 'ASMR life' every day, is still a good reminder for me. Not too long ago I was being interviewed for a documentary. Myself and the crew were in a very cosy and low-lit setting in my 'Tingle Shed' studio. The questions were in-depth and interesting to answer, and I was enjoying exploring my thoughts on the subjects and conversing with no time limit in a relaxed way. We'd been chatting for a while when the interviewer said something which at first caught me off-guard: 'But isn't it selfish to work on yourself all the time?' This isn't something I'd had cause ever to discuss in interviews. Straight away

I realised the interviewer already knew the answer but was just interested in my explanation of the subject, and it occurred to me that we all need reminders from time to time. I have touched on this already in the book; however, let me right now send a big distance hug and say it again: self-development, self-care and kindness is the number one most important job we have throughout our lives. However or whomever you are inside manifests itself in absolutely every aspect of your life, from how you think and how you behave to how you contribute to the world. I have heard it said so many times that living in service to others is the most fulfilling life there is and I wholeheartedly agree with this. But the only way to do that effectively and long term is to first nurture yourself to be the best you can. Be kind and patient with yourself and understand that there are many forms of strength. Sometimes the strongest among us are those who don't shout about it; they whisper and listen instead.

OK, let's have some ASMR moments together ...

Chapter 8

Your ASMR Day

ere are some steps to help you fill your day with little moments of ASMR, from the moment you wake up in the morning till you close your eyes at night. It's a way to 'feel' your day more, be present in your usual activities and find new ways to bring ASMR into your daily life.

You don't need to find any extra time to do these exercises. Do them all in one day or choose those that appeal to you most. They take longer to read than to actually complete, so don't feel overwhelmed; even building two or three minutes of an exercise into your day would be actioning positive change. Be proud of yourself that you are taking steps to be the best you can, and if you find that something just isn't working for you then try another method until you arrive at something with which you are comfortable. The most important thing is that by exploring possibilities you are trying new things and expanding your awareness.

Little moments to fill your day with ASMR

Perhaps read through the chapter before you get started to familiarise yourself with the theme and purpose of each exercise. It is the idea and intention behind each one that I would like you to take away, so feel free to adapt or change them around to best fit you and your own triggers or sensitivity. You may also practise the steps along to my voice using the audio version of this book. The steps can act as guided meditations to utilise however you wish.

Moment 1: Waking up with ASMR

This first exercise is to start your day. It can be done quite quickly, or steadily and slowly, depending on how busy your mornings usually are. If you would like to do this at another time of day, try it lying on your bed or sofa when you can find a quiet time. The focus of this moment is to wake up grounded, present, and to set your intention for the day ahead.

- As you begin to awaken, give yourself a moment to be still and quiet even before you open your eyes. Take a minute to hear your breathing and to feel the weight of your body on the mattress. Be quietly present in your space.

- Use your breathing to stay longer in this moment of not being fully awake yet. Keep your breaths long and even, breathing in through the nose and out through the mouth, or whatever is most comfortable for you.

- Begin to mentally explore the areas of your body as you sense them on the bed. Perhaps scan your body from the tips of your toes to the top of your head. As you arrive at your head, allow it to feel heavy and sink into the pillow. Now, follow that feeling of heaviness and calm all the way down your body – through your torso, arms and hands and then into your legs and feet. Visualise it flowing through your body.

- Sense the material beneath your body and note how it feels against your skin. Now, be aware of the duvet or sheet covering you. It may feel soft or textured. Heavy or light.

- Still in your sleepy and heavy state, slowly feel your way to opening your eyes. Allow them to adjust to the level of light around you. Before you begin to move your head, let your eyes wander around the room. Look at the things around you with fresh eyes, unattached to associations or emotions. Look at the shapes of any objects you can see, or how the light displays on the ceiling above you and the walls around you. Take a moment to properly observe this daily view that you rarely ever take the time to notice.

- Now turn your attention to listening. It might seem silent at first, but listen out for the smallest sounds – maybe from outside the window, like birdsong or distant traffic. Allow it to feel calming and reassuring. Perhaps there are sounds closer to you – from elsewhere in your home, or voices somewhere nearby. Allow them to be heard and accept they are there but distant from you, and they do not disturb your sense of calm and rest.

- Finally, focus on your sense of touch. Feel the sheets beneath you or the bedding covering you. Trace their weave lightly with your fingertips, noticing the sensation in your skin. Use the pads of your fingers and your nails too, if you like. Try alternate fingers to trace the patterns on the material.

- Repeat the patterns a few times, feeling the sensations change as your fingers become accustomed to the touch. Listen to the movements. Now add a little pressure to the bedding around you and feel the resistance against your fingers. Know that you are here and now. Feel the different areas of your body as you lie calmly in the bed.

- As you listen again for the sounds around you, notice how they fade into the background as you pick out one from the other. 'Play' the sounds using your awareness of them. You are surrounded by sensation and in control of your environment.

- Now is the time to set your intention for the day. Perhaps to start, you could take a word, such as 'joy' or 'love' or 'happiness' and decide to bring it into all of your interactions. Or you could be very specific and request something in detail from yourself. If you would like to set the intention to be open to something you would like to invite into your life, make sure it is a request from the heart and something *you* really want rather than something you think you *should* do. Also, have an active rather than a passive intention. Intend to be open to something you *do* want rather than something you *don't* want, e.g. 'I intend to invite joy into my life today and to bring it into all of my interactions with others.'

- You can finish by adding a simple smile to your face and feeling an 'inner smile' in response. Feel gratitude for what is about to come, knowing it is going to happen. This inner knowing will help you to manifest your intention.

Moment 2: Your ASMR Affirmation

Begin your day by affirming the positive to yourself. It helps to do this before any negative thoughts pop into your mind or when there is a quiet time early in your day. This can pre-empt any worries that might be about to take over and keep you focusing on the present. If you have time to sit in front of the mirror to do this then please do, or if looking at yourself in the mirror for too long is difficult at the moment, that's OK. Choose a picture on the wall that you like or a view from a window to look at instead; you can work your way up to looking at yourself later. If you are in a rush then you could do this exercise as you brush your teeth, apply make-up or dry your hair.

- Sit comfortably in front of a mirror, and look at yourself and smile. With a feeling of love, smile back to yourself. This can be odd at first. If it is easier, then imagine the person in the mirror is someone else and you are giving them a smile. You can come to the realisation that it is you later.

- If you have time, perhaps light some incense or a candle to add a nice scent and warmth around you. This provides a sense of ritual to support your daily affirmation.

- Now you are going to create your positive affirmation. Think of a statement that makes you feel stronger and more connected with your inner self. It is a truth that you know you need to tell yourself or hear out loud, a message from your heart and something that touches your deepest sense of what you need. For example, you could say:

  - I am strong and well.

  - I am proud of myself and what I am achieving in my life.

  - I love my body and the amazing things that it does for me.

  - Every day is a new opportunity to have a good day.

  - I am choosing to be happy today, because I am worthy of happiness.

  - I have abundance in my life and am grateful for everything.

  - I can build bridges and climb mountains with the love I have in my heart.

  - I see you, I accept you and I love you.

- Have a smile on your face, and absorb the view in front of you, or look into your own eyes in the mirror. Now, take three deep breaths and, as you do so, imagine your heart filling with positive energy each time as you repeat your chosen affirmation clearly five times. Speak it firmly and with kindness, either in your mind or out loud, keeping your body relaxed and smiling as you do so.

- Imagine your heart full of that positive energy and your body happy as you accept your positive message for the day ahead. Continue to look at yourself or your uplifting vision and breathe deeply. Now repeat the exercise again, before finishing.

- You can look for ways to repeat your affirmation throughout the day – ideally twice more at least. Find a private time in the middle of the day for this purpose in as quiet and calm a space as possible. And then repeat again before bed. Repetition is key to ensuring that your affirmation remains at the forefront of your mind and focuses your actions.

Moment 3: Your Morning Cup of Tea

For those who know me quite well already, you may be smiling now. It always comes down to tea, and in England EVERYTHING is made better with a nice hot cuppa. If you are not an utter freak for tea like me, then adapt this to your usual drink or other morning routine. As you now know, any simple task can be turned into an ASMR moment and meditative practice. Use regular daily activities as a chance to bring calm into your day. Here we are working with first tea and then toast.

- Start by selecting a mug or cup for your drink. Take the time to choose one that prompts a positive emotion – not just the closest to hand. Pick a cup with a shape or texture, colour or pattern that makes you happy. Perhaps it was a gift from a loved one, or has fun memories attached. When you have it in your hand, take some time to really look at it and feel it. Trace the patterns and colours with your fingertips and think about how they appeal to you and how they make you feel. It may be cold or warm in your hand. Rough or smooth. Heavy or light. Now run your hands over it, bringing all of your awareness at this moment to the cup. Turn on your kettle to boil the water.

- Take a teabag or some loose tea. Notice how the teabag or tea feels against your fingers. You may be able to smell the tea as you gently press it. Hear the soft crunching sound as you move the teabag, and let the loose tea fall around inside.

- Now turn back to the cup. Explore the sound of it. Tap it – gently at first, very carefully. Be aware of the sound and focus on it. Sometimes just one short tap can produce a soft ringing sound depending on the size of the room you are in. Take the time to see if you can 'feel' the sound anywhere in your body. Now tap more loudly and find a rhythm that feels comforting. Try playing around with the rhythm, fast and slow. Listen to the sounds and see if you can hear any harmonics (different notes) in the ringing.

- Now steadily pour the boiling water onto the tea. Listen to the pouring water and the sound as it reaches the tea. Note how the steam rises above the cup and disappears.

Sometimes there is a pleasant fizzing sound from the hot water hydrating the dried tea leaves. There may be warmth rising up from the cup to your face, and as you touch the cup feel the sensation of the heat on your fingers. Notice and be present in each movement – the bubbles, the steam and all the sounds.

- As you finish off the steps of your personal tea preparation, take a teaspoon and stir slowly. Listen to the gentle clink of the spoon against the cup and watch the movement of the water circling with the spoon.

- Lightly curl your hands around the cup and let the warmth spread into your hands. Focus on the drink and how it appeals to all of your senses. Observe all the feelings and emotions that may arise within you.

- Use this experience with toast to similarly explore and focus your senses in the here and now. Feel and smell the bread as you take it in your hands. Touch the harder edges and the softer centre and note the shape and texture. Feel its weight in your hands.

- Pop it into the toaster and note the warmth rising from the toaster as your bread starts to cook. Now select a plate for your toast. Again, choose a piece of crockery that appeals to you – with its colour, texture or shape. Feel its coolness beneath your fingertips and stroke its surfaces.

- Tap the surfaces gently to find the sound of the plate and play with the rhythm – faster and slower. Try tapping on different areas to make different sounds.

- When your toast is ready, note the warmth as you place it on your plate. Again, run your fingers over the surfaces and feel the crispness and rough texture.

- As you spread your toppings, listen to your knife scraping against the toast, backwards and forwards. Mindfully spread the toppings into all the corners of the toast, carefully and precisely covering it.

- Now enjoy your hot drink and toast. Be present and don't rush. Drink and eat slowly. Be grateful for what you have in front of you, and be aware of the different sensations within the process. Allow this simple task to fill you with calm and contentment.

Moment 4: An ASMR Daydream

This exercise is an opportunity to have a moment to rest in a dreamy state – something we do too infrequently. If you notice yourself drifting, it might be because you need a brain break. Daydreaming has been found to lower blood pressure and improve performance and working memory. We might normally do this while waiting in a queue or travelling on public transport, but here we are going to focus on doing it intentionally to give our mind and brain a rest during the day. When we are daydreaming we usually arrive in a theta brainwave state, which is the full state of relaxation before sleep, the meditative state. While in this state, we will also explore our connection with the senses using ASMR techniques.

If you are in a busy workplace and feel you would like to do this more discreetly, just choose the actions you are comfortable with. Otherwise, tell everyone about your daydream moment and perhaps they will do it too. The chances are that most of the people around you are too busy in their own minds to notice much anyway! Nevertheless, I will leave this with you to incorporate into your day as best you can.

- Sit yourself calmly before a picture, photograph or an object that you like or connect with – maybe a memorable image you've found online or a photo of somewhere you've visited. Choose somewhere that inspires strong imagery for you – scents of lemon trees, a vision of a stunning landscape or sounds from the sea. Perhaps it's somewhere you've always wanted to visit. Sit comfortably and focus on the image or object. Bring your awareness to your breathing, become calm and distance yourself from the business of your day. Allow yourself to drift into a daydream.

- Start by playing with a strand of your hair. Wind it gently around your fingers and feel the gentle pulling on your scalp. Feel the softness of the strands as well as their strength. Feel the pads of your fingers as you stroke your hair – be your own nurturing comforter. Close your eyes if it feels better to do so and allow your mind to drift to another happy image as you enjoy the movement. Don't rush the experience. Take time to fully immerse yourself in the sensation and try different ways of playing with your hair, finding out what is calming for you and increasing your response. Do not worry if unwanted thoughts pop into your mind. Just observe them coming in and refocus on the image you have in your mind, or open your eyes and focus again on the picture or object.

- Now, trace your forearm softly with the fingers of your hand, gliding them up and down for a few minutes. Again, notice the comforting touch and the warmth and love shown with each movement. Notice how soft your skin feels against your own hands – we all need this skin contact to be present in our bodies and to find a gentle, self-soothing touch that gives us the power to calm and comfort ourselves.

- Next, move your fingers to your neck and very lightly scratch slowly down from your hairline to your collarbone. Be aware of how your body supports you and protects you, and use this moment to be grateful for your body.

- Focus on the sensation and your breathing, slowly in and slowly out – and, as you are heavy, still and fully present in your body, allow your imagination to flow, observing the images and feelings that may arise.

- Now take a clean make-up brush and use it to softly brush over your face. Be light and slow. Brush your cheek, then slide it up and across your forehead. Run it lightly down the bridge of your nose. Brush in slow circular movements all around your face.

Use all three of these movements in your daydream or just one of them, whatever you would like. Just drift and explore your mental imagery and every sensation as it arises.

Sometimes in the theta state, we can experience processing of a past situation or emotional time in our life. This is normal – sometimes things come up that you forgot about a long time ago. Just go with the flow here and trust that it must be for a reason. Your mind just needed to work through something perhaps. It can help you find perspective about a situation that you may not find challenging any more but you did back then. When this happens for me I notice how much I have developed over the years and it helps me to let go of feelings I may be holding on to from the past.

Moment 5: An Object Connection

This exercise involves an item that is in your home or at work – something quite ordinary, perhaps a decorative object you haven't noticed for a while. Try not to choose a sentimental item or prized possession as we are not aiming to stir up too much thought or a complicated emotional response. We are going to use this object to see how anything can have ASMR 'properties' and to realise the beauty in things we already have. This helps us to change our perception, to understand that the joy that is in 'things' does not come from them being 'new' or 'fresh' but from their sensory properties. This connection can prompt and help us to see the existing beauty in ourselves and others.

- Choose your object. It could be a piece of ceramics, a favourite book, a small wooden bowl, an old piece of jewellery that you rarely wear, or a favourite jug or vase. Try to select something that you tend to walk past most days but do not stop to look at.

- Once you have your item, take a few deep breaths and focus your eyes on it. Take it in your hands and feel the textures of it against your fingers and palms. Continue your slow and steady breathing and, as you feel all the edges or curves of the object, bring your awareness to how you are feeling physically as well as emotionally.

- Images may pop into your mind. Watch them come in like pictures on a television screen and refocus your attention to bring to the object.

- Now explore the sound. Tap and scratch it lightly in different places and note the tones of the sounds. Use your nails and the pads of your fingers and hear the difference in sound.

- Notice the colours and move the object around to look at how the colour might change in the light. Often an object appears just one colour or texture but the reality is different when you look closer. Note the imperfections and other close-up details.

- Lift and place it against your cheek and feel the texture and temperature of it against your skin.

- Take a few minutes to properly observe this object using the textures, colours, sounds, smell and the visual 'feel' of it. Notice every physical response you may have throughout.

- 'Thank' the object and feel gratitude for it being with you, for being helpful or beautiful.

Taking the time to appreciate all the sensory aspects of this item and renew its value helps us to understand the worth in all the things that we have. It dampens the need for 'more' and any 'new', 'latest' things that our digital world can push us towards. It shows us also how to find the sensation in absolutely everything around us. Why not try to do this often with different objects, or when you feel the need for a shopping fix? Taking the time to stop and think about what we already have around us in our lives is a step towards happiness and contentment.

Moment 6: An ASMR Glass of Water

This is a little meditation exercise for you to add to your day whenever you can. Not only is it a mindful practice, it also adds more 'flavour' to the water and is a reminder to stay hydrated. All that is required is a glass, some water and you.

- Take an empty glass and hold it gently in your hands. Focus on the feel of the glass on your skin.

- Now close your eyes and breathe slowly in through your nose and out through your mouth three times – in through your nose and out through your mouth.

- Still with your eyes closed, release your hands from the sides of the glass and notice the sensation linger on your skin. Focus on this feeling for a while as you continue breathing.

- Now we will begin to make sounds on the glass. Very lightly tap the pads of your fingers on the surface and notice the sensation you feel through your fingertips. Run your fingers around the rim of the glass very lightly and feel the pressure on your skin.

- Use your nails to tap around the glass, making a gentle, light ringing sound. Listen and follow your intuition by making slower- and faster-paced sounds. Note any other ringing sounds you may hear as the sound waves bounce around the space you are in.

- Take your water and very slowly pour it into the glass. Look very closely at the flow of the water and the bubbles that form as you pour. Water loves to move – imagine all the happy little molecules sliding into the glass.

- Your body is made up of around 60 per cent water and soon the contents of this glass will be making you feel refreshed, forming new cells and renewing your body. Smile lightly to the water and project your gratitude towards it.

- Take the glass and move it towards your lips. Keeping your eyes focused on the glass, notice the movement of your arm and the weight in your hand.

- As you drink the water, be present in the feeling of the water filling your mouth and flowing into your body.

- Place the glass down, being sure to feel the texture beneath your fingertips. Notice the lightness of it again and take a long, refreshed deep breath, in through your nose and out through your mouth.

Moment 7: ASMR Your Nightly Routine

Here we can enhance your nightly routine by including some ASMR techniques. Use this regular activity to clear your mind and become present, ground yourself and add some positivity before finally being ready for sleep. It is also a good time to feel gratitude for the day you have just experienced, and an opportunity to reconnect your mind and body. Once you know what triggers work best for you, you can tailor this moment to your own preferences and perhaps come up with some ideas of your own. I will use the activities that most of us do before bed as examples.

- In the bathroom before cleaning your teeth, take a short moment to connect with yourself in the mirror. Look at yourself for a while if you can and recognise the essence of yourself. By this I mean to look into your eyes and come to the knowing of who you are rather than just the surface image. Again, this may be difficult for some; it is normal for this to be strange if you are not used to doing it or happen to be struggling with any issues at this time. If this is the case, perhaps just gaze at something near to the mirror and notice your reflection in your peripheral vision, to see yourself out of the corner of your eye.

- As you look into your eyes and see your 'self', come to the awareness of your breathing. Breathe deeply, noticing both the sensation of the air entering your body and the sound of the breath.

- Draw your awareness to the rest of your body and take a moment to loosen up any clenched muscles. Perhaps visualise a brief body scan to make sure you are not tense anywhere.

- Pick up your toothbrush and be aware of this moment. You are about to clean your teeth. It is very easy for the mind to wander and begin to worry when we do these simple and regular activities. To stop this we can use the objects and the sensations they produce to keep us present, to find something more interesting in them and not be bored and wander into worry or anxiety. Feel the bristles of your toothbrush against your fingertips. Notice the colour and the shapes in the movement of the toothpaste as you spread it over the top, hear the sound of the cap on the toothpaste as it closes and opens.

- When you brush, be sure to draw your awareness to every sensation of the bristles on your teeth and the sound of the brushing. If there is other activity around you or other sounds and they don't require your attention, just keep your focus on this sound only.

- As you finish by turning off the tap and placing your brush back in its holder, perhaps you wash and dry your face afterwards. While doing this, ground yourself at the same time. Be aware of your feet on the ground and visualise them firmly in place. Draw a nice warm feeling up through the soles of your feet and through your legs into your body. Feel still and in your body, here and now.

- As you pick up any cream or lotions for your face, be totally present in every step. Notice how the bottle sounds when you open the cap, or the crinkling of the cotton-wool packet and the feel of the cotton wool in your fingers.

- As you apply your face cream, lotion or oils, try tapping around your face lightly, with feathery fingers drifting over your skin using different speeds and weight of pressure. The lighter you keep it, the more 'tingly' it can be. Be aware of your breathing again; slowly in through your nose and out through your mouth. You might even like to use the 4–7–8 breathing technique from Chapter 7 here. (Look up different breathing techniques online to see if any are right for you.)

- Once your cream has absorbed and your hands are dry, take a moment to give yourself an ASMR hair 'treatment'. Use your nails to gather little sections of hair around your hairline, very lightly scratching and gathering the little short hairs around the front. Run the palms of your hands over the top of your head, barely touching your hair. Take tiny sections of hair and tug very gently till you feel the lightest sensation on your scalp. Close your eyes if it helps to draw all your attention to the sensations in your scalp, and feel the hair on your fingers too.

- Finally, as you are looking at yourself in the mirror, be sure to mentally congratulate yourself on a job well done in your day. Feel proud of yourself for what you have achieved and focus on the moments that made you feel good, that connected you to who you are and how you might have manifested your intention and affirmation for the day.

Being an ASMRtist I often imagine filming myself doing some of these steps (which I often have, of course). It may sound a little odd but imagining all the steps one at a time, and all the aspects of each step and how it could sound and feel to watch, actually keeps me very present. Perhaps there is something in your night-time routine that you know would be a good ASMR trigger and you can imagine you are making a video of it for someone else. I am often told by viewers that their children do this after watching ASMR videos – they make believe they are creating their own. It's lovely to know they are enjoying this playful and natural yet mindful practice. You can bring this out in yourself too.

Moment 8: Ready to Sleep

Time to fall asleep ASMR-style. Hopefully you will have been able to include some of the earlier moments in your day so far and they have helped you to achieve a calmer state as you arrive at this moment before sleep. Chapter 6 has advice about using ASMR for sleep, so do look back at that as well.

This moment contains the use of your preferred video content. Before we start, it is helpful to plan ahead which video(s) you are going to use that evening and stay with it, rather than using this time to search around for others. Remember, this is your relaxation and sleep time, so use the content for that purpose and do any active searching during the day. This is when a playlist or downloaded content can be useful. Use it as a deliberate therapy rather than a distraction to get lost online.

Here we are, time to fall asleep …

Make yourself comfortable for bedtime. A cooler temperature in the room is known to be helpful, and remember that warmer lighting is better for you at night. Enjoy your bedtime environment and fill it with things that bring you joy. Use aromatherapy oils if this will help you to relax. Consider the textures, smells and colours of your surroundings as much as you are able, so that this space is a calm haven for you.

Know that this is only the time you have designated for your sleep. Rather than focus on the time by when you would like to fall asleep, remove any demands on yourself and see this as your 'sleep window'. Relaxing in bed is still resting and very important and healing too.

- Once you are in bed, become present in your space and feel the weight of your body sink into the mattress. Take a few long, deep breaths, filling your body with air. Close your eyes and listen to the sound of your breathing, in through your nose and out through your mouth.

- Now, as your body is becoming ready for sleep, you may want to spend some time experiencing some ASMR content. Perhaps dim the screen on your device, warm up the colour and watch a video wearing headphones, or without. Immerse yourself in the visuals, the sound and all the physical sensations they bring for you.

- Let go and allow your breathing to become automatic as you focus on the elements in the video: the sounds, the movements, the colours and your connection in this moment with the content creator. Allow your body to take over, to just be present, heavy and at peace.

- As you feel your eyelids become heavy, this is the time to allow yourself to fall asleep. If you are sitting up then place your device to your side and lay your head down. You may turn everything off, focus on your breathing and fall asleep. Or if you would like to keep the sound going then let it play in the background. However you are able or like to sleep while listening is up to you.

- Close your eyes, bring your awareness to the softness of your breathing and drift away into a peaceful night's sleep.

- Goodnight, sleep tight :-)

However you like to experience content before sleep is entirely your preference. The most important thing is that you are aware of how to use it, and don't allow the device or the hosting website of the content to take over your relaxation and sleep time. If you need to have a separate smaller device with some downloaded content and a speaker in your room, then do that to help take away temptation. Whatever works positively for you is right.

A little 'mum advice' from me is to have plants in your room that are known to absorb the electromagnetic frequencies that our electrical devices give off, (common choices are cactus and snake plant) and try not to keep your device right by your head while you sleep.

If you happen to wake during the night and would like to get back to sleep, just repeat the process. Being kind and patient with yourself is the most important thing.

Other moments for ASMR

Let's consider other times in your day when *feeling* and *being* would be more helpful to you than giving your mind space to get up to mischief. Remember, your mind is a tool for thinking when it is needed. When it is not, this is a time for feeling and being in our environment, or one we create for ourselves that is calming.

When you walk from one place to another, be aware of your footsteps, the freshness of the air, and look for the beauty around you. When you are waiting in a queue, use that time for listening and grounding yourself in the moment. When you travel to and from places, see it as a time to explore your senses and be present on the journey, noticing everything in front of you. If you are driving this can be particularly helpful, especially if you take the same route each day. It helps to stop your mind from wandering and to focus on the car and the road; be present on the journey.

When you pick up things to use them, focus on the sensation of the items in your hands and feel the texture of them. Explore the sounds of things you use every day. Always be aware that once your mind begins to wander to something that doesn't serve you well, you can bring your awareness back to your senses using sound, touch and self-soothing actions.

Explore the use of video and sound content to enhance your day and night, never as a distraction *from* yourself but as a useful tool for focus, calm, exploring physical sensation and a brain break – a tool to bring you *to* yourself. ASMR is an exciting form of mindfulness using sounds, physical sensations, community and connection. I hope these guided moments are helpful in bringing it more into your daily life.

Testimonies and Personal Stories

Annie Wright, clinical therapist, Evergreen Counseling, California

My name is Annie Wright, LMFT and I'm a clinical therapist and the founder of a therapy center called Evergreen Counseling which serves Millennial, Gen-Z, and Gen-X aged clients here in the California Bay Area.

As a therapist who specializes in working with complex relational trauma (meaning trauma experienced in relationships and usually in early childhood), I often have a need to recommend and suggest various self-soothing tools to my clients for their use in between therapy sessions to help reduce their emotional distress.

One of the tools I discovered that can be highly effective for individuals who are struggling with anxiety, depression, and other mood disorders is listening to and watching ASMR videos by several trusted ASMR artists.

In my clinical experience, ASMR videos, because they trigger a calming and soothing physiological response in many clients, can be an effective self-soothing tool.

It's notable, too, that for my clients who have a history of childhood neglect, abandonment, and maltreatment, 'special attention' ASMR videos – whether this is hair brushing, scalp massage, reading a story or tucking someone into bed – not only have a relaxing response, but, for some clients, they can also provide what I call a 'reparative experience' – a corrective emotional experience that provides them with something they didn't get and were longing for in their early life.

The combination of this – a reparative experience plus a relaxation response – makes ASMR videos a supportive adjunct tool to the work of therapy for many of my clients.

Annie Wright, LMFT is the founder and clinical director of Evergreen Counseling – a therapy center located in Berkeley, California – as well as a licensed psychotherapist who specializes in complex relational trauma. She's also a published writer with pieces and opinions appearing in and on Forbes, NBC, The Huffington Post, *Buzzfeed*, Reader's Digest *and more. You can find her online at* www.anniewrightpsychotherapy.com *or at* www.evergreencounseling.com

Amy, ASMR viewer, Scotland

I first found ASMR in 2010 when I was going through a particularly stressful time in my life. I was under pressure at uni, working in a job that I absolutely hated and was suffering badly from depression. This was only exaggerated by crippling insomnia that I was experiencing at the same time and I was at a loss as to what to do to get out of the cycle of bad sleep and feeling down.

One night I searched for 'relaxation videos' on YouTube and after a few clicks I found my first 'ASMR' video which was by Maria GentleWhispering. At first, like many, I thought it was a little strange but it really helped distract and calm my mind. It was through Maria's recommendation that I found Emma. Her warm personality immediately drew me in and I have watched her videos every night since. Watching these videos helped me break out of my unhealthy sleeping pattern and finally get a good night's rest. Being able to sleep and having that time to feel relaxed was like a magic cure for my depression and insomnia. After a few weeks I noticed a huge improvement in my mood, I finally felt positive again. I got up the courage to quit my job and enjoy life for the first time in months.

Since then I have watched ASMR videos every single night. It has helped me enormously. Not only do I find inspiration in ASMR artists like Emma, but ASMR helps me manage my anxiety, helps me sleep and generally manage my own mental health in a really positive way.

I watched ASMR videos the night before my wedding to calm my nerves, it has got me through two house moves, job interviews, illnesses, bereavements and most recently a really difficult pregnancy and labour.

I suffered from SPD – which is chronic hip pain in pregnancy. This made it extremely difficult to sleep but watching and listening to ASMR helped me relax and take my mind off of the pain for a while.

During my pregnancy I researched and went to classes for hypnobirthing. It takes weeks, if not months, to get your mind ready to do this successfully but I realised that I had actually trained my brain in a very similar way already through watching ASMR videos for so many years. I knew that I could use ASMR videos alongside the hypnobirthing tapes when I was in labour to relax because I had already created those associations in my mind with calmness and relaxation.

I can honestly say that it worked great for me. I was in labour for 33 hours (it ended in an emergency C-section) but in that time I watched all my favourite ASMR videos and I surprised myself with how well it helped me cope with the pain. Having the familiarity of ASMR made me feel more in control of the situation and I even told the midwife all about ASMR and showed her a couple of videos.

I now have my beautiful baby boy who is the joy of my life and I find myself whispering and doing 'ASMR' sounds to him at night before he goes to sleep. His favourite is when I repeat, 'It's okay, shhh.' He also likes tapping sounds and loves it when I gently brush my fingers down over his eyes. I love being able to use what I've picked up from ASMR videos in real life with him. I truly treasure that 20 minutes every night when we have a cuddle and wind down. I hope that as he grows up he will continue to be able to find relaxation in sound and touch the same way I have done and when he's older we can cuddle up and watch some videos together. Especially the ones Emma makes for children.

Now that I'm a mum, I hardly ever get any 'me' time and it feels like I'm constantly busy but I still take time out at night to lie in bed with my baby beside me, holding his little hand and watch ASMR. This time is so important to me because it lets me switch off and sort of 'recharges' my positivity for the next day. It helps me cope with the stresses of parenthood, particularly in the early days when my son suffered from colic and would cry for hours on end.

ASMR has been a constant source of positivity in my life for so long now and I am forever grateful for the sense of calm it has given me and the ability to stay on top of my anxiety – it has worked better for me than any medication.

I feel like I have a real bond with ASMRtists like Emma, even though I only watch her through a screen and she has no idea who I am, she has been the most reliable friend to me through the most difficult and important times of my life.

I see ASMR as a form of self-care, in the same category as going for a massage or facial or having reiki. As more research is done into ASMR, I hope that misconceptions continue to be diminished and more people start to understand the true benefits it can have on mental health.

Megan, ASMR viewer, Arizona, US

During the spring of 2013 I discovered the warm, calming, and seemingly unelicited, spine-tingling feeling I've experienced nearly all my life finally had a name, Autonomous Sensory Meridian Response, or more commonly known as ASMR. I came across the name completely by accident. I was going through an incredibly difficult time. All within the month of May, my grandfather, with whom I was very close, had passed away after a long battle with cancer. My then fiancé had decided to end our engagement and subsequently our relationship. I withdrew from the nursing program I had been enrolled in and began to question the very direction of my life. I felt lost and the weight of my devastation and grief made me feel unspeakably sad. I began to have an impossible time sleeping. I'd be up night after night with a mind that wouldn't shut off. I would take naps here and there, but the sleep deprivation only fed my depressive state. One night, out of pure desperation, I logged onto YouTube, searched for 'videos for sleep', and countless videos popped up. I went through any and all of them hoping to find one that would help. One night I stumbled across a clip from a Bob Ross episode and as I listened to his calm, quiet voice and watched him softly stroke the canvas with his paint brush the warm tingling feeling I had felt often as a child melted over my head and down my spine. It had been years since I had felt that feeling. In childhood I remember there were simple pleasures that seemed to bring this feeling; dipping my hand into the barrel of dried beans at the grocery store, my mother gently scratching my back, or hearing my dad flip through the pages of his law books as he studied after we were put to bed at night. I allowed the tingles to envelope me and I drifted to sleep.

Over the next few weeks I looked for more clips of *The Joy Of Painting* with Bob Ross episodes to help me sleep, and as I did, I stumbled across content producers creating something called ASMR. I watched videos of people speaking softly, gently creating sounds with various objects, performing roleplays, and tenderly whispering into microphones. With video after video I was feeling the sweet tingly feeling we all adore, and little by little I felt myself returning to how I was before I felt so traumatized. I felt like I was being healed with love and kindness relayed through ASMR. I learned to arm myself with the calm and collected feeling I experienced while watching the videos and apply it when I needed it throughout my days. I learned to breathe, I learned to reflect, and I learned to accept and meditate. I learned I could be strong and gentle without jeopardizing myself. Most of all, I learned that if I could feel love from complete strangers through a screen and experience healing from it then I felt I could definitely do the same for my patients in person.

I feel ASMR not only has been an invaluable tool to enlighten me during a very dark time in my life, but it has also become a method of practice for me. I work as a nurse's aide in a Neurological Intensive Care Unit and I'm currently in my last year of nursing school. I bring as much of what I see in ASMR videos as I can into my practice of caring for people. Maybe I am biased, but I see a difference in my patients. Most of them have injuries in their brains caused by many different ailments, but all result in a sensitivity to stimuli. Even though they're mostly sedated, they still react to sound and to touch. I've noticed the care provided is less stressful and better received when I mimic methods in ASMR videos. I verbalize and describe everything I'm doing. I make sure my voice is soft, warm, and I speak quietly. Every touch and movement are gentle and methodical. I provide words of encouragement and reassurance and allow for certain therapeutic sounds to be experienced: gentle dripping of water in a basin, crinkling of paper packaging, or quiet tapping on tissue boxes. Though I'm not a physician and I have no scientific explanation for the observed reaction of my patients, I do know the outcome is my patients are calmed and comforted. In nursing school they've taught us that nursing is both a science and an art. For me, the artistic side of the care that I have provided and will continue to provide my patients will be expressed through nurturing of the human element shown to me through ASMR.

Stephanie Romiszewski, sleep physiologist, Sleepyhead Clinic, Exeter, UK

I'm a sleep physiologist and the founder of Sleepyhead Clinic, working with people around the world struggling with sleep disorders and issues in my own clinic and for our National Health Service. I also run a sleep research group which primarily looks at sleep education in the UK. I work with the evidence-based and approved sleep medicine behavioural techniques that can treat insomnia long term.

I first heard of ASMR when I visited a friend who was listening to it while he was doing his design work. There was whispering in the background and I asked what it was. He found it helped him to concentrate and I found it relaxing. I already love nature sounds for relaxing so theoretically speaking I could understand how certain sensory stimuli can help you feel calm, and that this might be different for everyone. This is not such a new phenomenon.

My work relies on me making science accessible to the public, and making the gold standard treatment options work for them in their everyday lives. I am constantly adapting the science to meet the ever-changing needs of a 24/7 society which relies heavily on technology, something that doesn't always go hand in hand with sleep. I've heard about ASMR a lot more through my clients now, as its popularity rises and initial research into the fields show some interesting findings.

I'm careful to be clear that as far as we know at this point in time, ASMR cannot fix a sleep disorder like insomnia, just as relaxation and anxiety reduction alone cannot do this (as any person suffering with chronic insomnia will tell you). But if ASMR helps someone feel a little less anxious, a little safer and a little less lonely at night time, especially when trying to implement a behavioural sleep intervention (which, just like long term weight loss, can be a challenge), this can only be a good thing. These are crippling symptoms that can make sleep problems worse after all.

Further information can be found at:

sleepyheadclinic.co.uk

Amy Matthews, comedian and ASMR viewer, UK

I'm a stand-up comedian, and ASMR has played a strangely important role in managing the weird working hours and emotionally demanding nature of the job.

The first 'tingles' I ever had as a child was when my Nan tickled my back and arms with her long nails until I fell asleep. I attended Deeksha meditation sessions at university, where Deeksha-givers would hover their hands around your head and shoulders to transfer energy whilst you meditated. This is a sensation I find very similar to watching hand movement videos. I remember the first time I watched an ASMR video, I felt the odd static-like feeling come through the screen.

I couldn't believe I could get the same feeling by just watching and listening to specific movements and sounds. Tapping, crinkles, whispering and hand movements are my favourite. I like anything with these crisp, sound qualities as I get misophonia [dislike of certain sounds] from eating sounds or 'wet' noise.

A stand-up gig is rarely completely 'flat'. There tends to be a real high after a good one, and a low after a bad one, and regardless of how the gig itself goes, the bit before (be it the minute before getting on stage or the morning of the gig itself) tends to be anxiety-inducing. In summary, it's a job that tugs you to and from the poles of positive and negative emotion, and riddles you with anxiety on the journey in between. ASMR has helped me stabilise these extremes.

Whether I'm wanting to forget a gig that just happened or wanting to calm down after the adrenaline rush of a good one, the chances are it's extremely late to be going to bed either way. In the same way as anyone in an industry that works anti-social hours, getting in to bed late is one thing and switching off enough to go to sleep is another. I almost always listen to ASMR before bed. In my experience, most people in my generation – not comics specifically, but everyone – has to listen to something before bed, be it a podcast, radio, music or leaving the TV on. We're so hyperstimulated that I think the quiet before bed is actually unnerving and jarring for lots of people my age (in their twenties), and perversely actually keeps us awake. I find that for me, ASMR bridges that gap; I'm not keeping myself awake by watching television or engaging with a podcast, but I have just enough audio-visual engagement to ease my mind. I used to listen to white noise, but where ASMR excels is it transcends mere 'distraction' and enters into active, quasi-physical soothing. Rather than simply occupying my subconscious, it triggers the calming phenomenon of tingles and haptic sensation. Moreover, if engaged by ASMR, I'm less likely to be tackling 'shower thoughts' at 2am – you know the 'How different would my life be if my parents had named me differently?' and the 'What photo would they use on the news if I went missing?'.

There's a sense of authentic escapism that comes with watching or listening to ASMR. It carves out time and space to concentrate on something and nothing all at once. Your mind is focussed on something that asks nothing of you, which in modern social and digital environs is very rare. ASMR videos, at a base level, permit us time to switch off from the day, but where it truly benefits me is not just its ability to carve out headspace and relaxation, but give actual comfort and recalibrate the senses. Sometimes in comedy you need more than just relaxation, and seek actual reassurance, which can be found in so many roleplay or affirmation ASMR videos. In a job so reliant on approval from strangers, there's something stabilising and hopeful about connection with and assurance from ASMRtists.

Markus, ASMR viewer, Texas, US

My name is Markus. I'm a 30-year-old male living in the United States. We, unlike many others, are blessed to live in a place where people have the freedom to make their lives as they see fit, with easy access to food, water, technology and education. Fortunate as we are, life still somehow manages to be filled with stress, troubles and worries on a day-to-day basis – surprise expenses, challenges at work, bumps in the long road that is a committed relationship, etc. So often we forget to stop and enjoy life as we hustle to get through to the next day and keep bills and other important payments up to date, hours going by spent texting and watching TV, never stopping to wonder if we actually know who we are as people, and the true characters of the people we surround ourselves with. Time goes by so quickly when you're stuck in a state of just 'existing' – attention on every small screen and thoughts in every place but the present. I used to lay awake at nights, tossing and turning over every little thing – with no skill or knowledge of how to calm myself down or find a sense of stillness. It was in this frustrating quagmire of 'existing' and not 'living' that I auspiciously discovered ASMR – and subsequently Emma.

Since watching ASMR, I found I was not only enjoying a carefully planned and executed ASMR experience – done with professionalism and love. I was also being educated. I learned through regular viewing every day that there is more to life than keeping your head down and dashing through. It is important to find serenity and harmony, and know where you fit in this world, and the worlds of those around you. Through using the videos, I found myself changing, and more often I found myself stopping and just 'being in the present'. It's both odd and sad to say the feeling of just 'stopping to smell the roses' was completely foreign to this competitive capitalist American, but I loved it. I began to actively seek it out.

The difficult act of loving oneself is an act so frequently neglected as we struggle so hard to please those around us. As I indulged in my interests, I gained knowledge I would not have otherwise had, and focused on taking better care of myself a bit more each day. I admit that my mind was abuzz and struggled to adapt as I sat in silence and contemplated how it was I really felt about things going on my life. I had grown so used to the noise of TVs, phones and computers running as background noise every hour of every day that 'quiet' almost felt anxious at times. But with a bit of discipline and practice, time began to slow down, and I truly became a calmer, kinder and more relaxed individual. I stopped trying to control every aspect of my life, understanding that not everything is up to me, and that some things are better left as mysteries. There's a contradictory and paradigm-shifting sense of freedom to be had in surrendering the desire to control every part of one's life.

Over the past couple of years the change in me has been so drastic that even my parents and my friends had noticed and began to question my newfound glow of positivity and calm demeanor, and how I seemed to be physically getting younger. (I had lost excess weight and my thinning hair and dry skin started looking healthier). I've built new bridges in my relationship, and by returning to a simpler time of real and honest communication – without electronics to get in the way and distract us from truly listening to each other – we feel closer and more in love than ever. I've found out things about the person I've been living with for years that I had never known before. It was like meeting him for the first time again; it's amazing how many things pass us by because we simply don't make time to have a real conversation. I even went so far as to completely redecorate my home with warmer and brighter colors to reflect this new love for life and the true happiness in my heart. I now recognize each new day for the exciting journey that it is, and by focusing more in the present, I found that almost all aspects of my life within my control have improved.

Sara Benincasa, author and ASMR viewer, US

I'm an author, and I write frequently about managing anxiety. This does not, however, make me an anxiety expert or someone who is adept at chilling out. A few years ago, I began to have trouble falling asleep at night.

I was dealing with a difficult romantic relationship and an alcohol problem that had slowly begun to worsen. I was not always a kind or thoughtful partner or friend in those days, and the guilt kept me up some nights as much as the general unhappiness. I discovered ASMR videos, which helped me get to sleep without the assistance of bourbon. In fact, I learned some self-soothing tips from ASMR videos – new visualization exercises, new breathing techniques, DIY approaches to aroma-therapy and massage.

I'm 38 now, and ASMR videos have helped me through a cross-country move, through breakups, through the death of my beloved grandmother, through illness, through the first year without alcohol, through my adjustment to working with an addiction therapist, through my tentative and halting entry into a sobriety program I would eventually embrace, and through worries about career and family and friends and love.

But ASMR isn't just for those who are having a rough time. I have a lovely life, and am grateful for so many things. I don't watch ASMR every night, but when I do, it isn't necessarily on a tough night. ASMR videos are wonderfully weird and just plain fun to watch.

I've learned over time that meditation, medication, proper nutrition, talk therapy, exercise, my sobriety program and sleep are my best friends in managing a happier or at least healthier life, but I am always delighted to add something new to my toolkit. And that's exactly why I'm so grateful for ASMR videos like the ones Emma makes.

sarabenincasa.com

Kristin Atherton, actress and audio book reader, London, UK

I experienced ASMR (though I honestly had no earthly idea that's what it was) from a very young age – around age four or five. Appropriately enough (given my current career) it was all thanks to an audio book and the gorgeous voice of Una Stubbs. She was the narrator for my favourite set of books, *My Naughty Little Sister*, and there was something about her whispery but crisp tone of voice that was just so enjoyable, calming and – that all important ASMR word – tingly! But it wasn't until about five years ago I realised that feeling wasn't unique to me, and that it had a name. A friend was talking about watching YouTube ASMR videos and when she described the feeling I was delighted; not just that other people got 'tingles' but that there was a whole online community where I could find ASMR triggering material. After that conversation I went straight on to YouTube and found my first ASMRtist (whose videos I'm still a fan of today).

I'm quite an anxious person and I often find it hard not to always be 'active' or 'doing something'. Whether I'm on holiday or at home, I always find projects and tasks and I don't find relaxing comes easily to me. Watching

ASMR videos is the exception; without them I sometimes don't know how I would calm myself down after a long day. If I'm feeling stressed or having trouble sleeping, watching even thirty minutes of my favourite ASMRtist normally does the trick.

In my career as an actor and audiobook reader, I'm so aware of the power of voice. Listening to an audiobook or an ASMR video is so intimate; such a uniquely one-on-one experience. When I'm recording an audiobook it always helps me to think I'm telling the story to just one person, and I know that that's the appeal of a lot of ASMR material – personal attention and a soothing intimacy. Also, if I'm on my way to a stressful audition or in the middle of a busy set with lots going on around me, ten or so minutes on YouTube with my favourite ASMRtist will normally put me in the exact right (calm) headspace to get the job done.

Georgie, legal professional and ASMR viewer, England

I am a Law and French graduate from the University of Bristol, currently working at The European Court of Justice in Luxembourg. This summer I was delighted to have been called to the Bar of England and Wales, which means that I am one step closer to fulfilling my dream of practicing as a Barrister in Public and Human Rights Law.

I first experienced ASMR as a child from real-life 'triggers', such as having my hair twisted into a bun before dancing, using whispered voices with friends whilst playing with Sylvanian Families or listening to the rain patter on the roof of our mobile classroom at primary school. During my A-levels in around 2011, when I first started participating in 'moots' (mock trials), to help with stress and nerves I started watching 'soft spoken' tutorial videos which gradually emerged as the ASMR community.

As a lawyer/linguist, I have moved for work and study between England and continental Europe at least once a year over the last 7 years. Although this lifestyle comes with excitement, it can make me feel uprooted, impacting my sleep and ability to settle into new places. ASMR has supported me greatly through these adjustment periods, bringing me nostalgia and comfort.

The last year of my vocational training has been the most challenging and listening to ASMR has helped me through difficult periods by keeping me grounded. As a lawyer, or any academic professional, it is easy to lose that grounding, even when working in person-centred areas of law such as crime, human rights and family law. Engaging in mindfulness and taking breaks from work to meditate or listen to ASMR not only relieves stress and pressure but also brings a human focus back to your work. Putting in my earphones, closing my eyes and listening to ASMR is the best way to calm my nerves and keep focused before practising oral pleadings in front of a judge. I am incredibly grateful for the work and creativity of the ASMR community.

Matt, ASMRtist, Articulate Design ASMR

As somebody who doesn't experience the physical response associated to ASMR, I'm often asked how I stumbled onto this seemingly new-found phenomenon, and how it might still be beneficial to me. I've always found particular scenes from movies to be really relaxing, any kind of monologue or softly spoken dialect, so one day I decided to make a playlist on YouTube with lots of these kinds of clips and have it playing as I went to fall sleep. Very quickly, YouTube was able to understand the kinds of videos I was searching for and one day recommended an ASMR video. After clicking, I immediately knew I'd found something incredible, a tool that no matter how stressed I was, or how much my brain might be dwelling on work or day-to-day things that needed doing, just offered a natural distraction from them and enabled my mind to focus on something other than the busy chatter that a worried brain churns through.

ASMR comes in all forms and offerings and while still establishing itself as a medium, I always like to compare it to something like photography. You can take pictures of mountains, rivers, sunsets, selfies and weddings – and no matter what you capture, it's still classed as photography. However, the content of course can change dramatically from person to person or camera to camera. The same can be said for ASMR. Some find the simple tapping sounds to be relaxing, others find medical check-up role plays to be particularly helpful as they simulate that soothing, reassuring doctor presence. Seeing any kind of ASMR video for the first time, without the context of relaxation in mind, can seem very unusual and confusing. This is understandable and this opinion won't be changed overnight, but for every day ASMR is watched and listened to, millions of people around the world are sleeping easier, panicking less and feeling less isolated.

Regardless of which kind of videos I choose to view, ASMR content at its very core is designed and created with relaxation in mind – a judgement-free space that reminds the listener that they're safe, considered and valued. Even if you're in a perfect place mentally and just need to get a good night's sleep, an ASMR video is a free, non-medicated sleep aid that distracts and relaxes, effortlessly. After watching the videos to relax and sleep, I decided to become more involved in the community and make my own videos. I enjoy contributing to the relaxation of others now and have made many friends by being a creator myself.

Further Reading and Research

ASMR: The Sleep Revolution by Benjamin Nichols (2017, Createspace)

Why We Sleep: The New Science of Sleep and Dreams by Matthew Walker (2017, Allen Lane)

Dr Andrew Weil and the 4-7-8 breathing technique can be found at: www.youtube.com/watch?v=_-C_VNM1Vd0

Research articles

Poerio GL, Blakey E, Hostler TJ, Veltri T, More than a feeling: Autonomous sensory meridian response (ASMR) is characterised by reliable changes in affect and physiology, *PLoS ONE* 13(6):e0196645 doi. org/10.1371/journal.pone.0196645

Barratt, EL, Davis NJ, Autonomous Sensory Meridian Response (ASMR): a flow-like mental state, (2015) *PeerJ* 3:e851 *peerj.com/articles/851*

McErlean AJ, Banissy MJ, Assessing individual variation in personality and empathy traits in self-reported autonomous sensory meridian response, *Multisensory research* 30(6):601–613 www.researchgate.net/publication/317247907

Lochte BC, Guillory SA, Richard CAH, Kelley WM, An fMRI investigation of the neural correlates underlying the autonomous sensory meridian response (ASMR) *Bioimpacts* 2018; 8(4): 295–304. www.ncbi.nlm.nih.gov/pmc/articles/PMC6209833/

Hertenstein MJ, Keltner D, App B, Bulleit BA, Jaskolka AR, Touch communicates distinct emotions, *Emotion* 2006 Aug 6(3):528–33 www.depauw.edu/learn/lab/publications/documents/touch/2009_Touch_The_communication_of_emotion_via_touch.pdf

Uvnäs-Moberg K, Handlin L, Petersson M, Self-soothing behaviours with particular reference to oxytocin release induced by non-noxious sensory stimulation, *Front Psychol* 2015 Jan 12(5):1529 www.ncbi.nlm.nih.gov/pubmed/25628581

Acevedo BP, Aron EN, Aron A, Sangster M-D, Collins N, Brown LL, The highly sensitive brain: an fMRI study of sensory processing sensitivity and response to others' emotions, *Brain Behav* 2014 Jul 4(4):580–594 www.ncbi.nlm.nih.gov/pubmed/25161824

Desek JA, Benson H, A model of the comparitive clinical impact of the acute stress and relaxation responses, *Minn Med* 2009 May 92(5):47–50 www.ncbi.nlm.nih.gov/pmc/articles/PMC2724877/

Ardiel EL, Rankin CH, The importance of touch in development, *Paediatr Child Health* 2010 Mar 15(3):153 www.ncbi.nlm.nih.gov/pubmed/21358895

Lipton B, The Jump From Cell Culture to Consciousness, *Integr Med (Encinitas)* 2017 Dec 16(6): 44–50 *www.ncbi.nlm.nih.gov/pmc/articles/PMC6438088*

Chevalier G, Sinatra ST, Oschman JL, Sokal, K, Sokal P, Earthing: Health implications of reconnecting the human body to the earth's surface electrons *J Environ Public Health* 2012: 291541 *www.ncbi.nlm.nih.gov/pmc/articles/PMC3265077*

Acknowledgements

This book is for everyone who has ever commented under a video or social media post of mine or ever written to me. For all of the kind thoughts I thank you from the bottom of my heart. Though it sometimes takes me a while to see all the messages, especially private ones, I read and digest every word. For every paragraph in this book there are hundreds of comments behind it, giving me the courage, confidence and strength to write it. You are all so important to me, and I thank you very much for being openly and publicly kind to one another.

I would like to thank everyone in the ASMR community – long-term members and new – for being brave, loving and strong in their lives each day. Your kindness and sensitivity really does have the power to change the world.

To my ASMRtist friends: there is a certain freedom in being seen as the weird one in the room and we wear that badge gracefully. To have the strength to remain patient and strong when others mock what they don't understand means we're a loving force to be reckoned with. For those of us who have been around for a long time, we have experienced a lot and smiled the whole way through. I am so very proud of all of us, especially now that ASMR is more understood and continues to be a useful form of comfort and healing for so many. Everything I do to support ASMR is for all of us, this book included, and I really hope that I have done a good job in explaining what we do. I love you all – not one of us could do this half as effectively without the whole. Thank you for everything.

A big hug of acknowledgement goes out to Olivia Morris and Kate Latham and the rest of the Unwind Your Mind team. Olivia has total belief in ASMR as a therapeutic tool and has been watching for a long time, waiting for the right time to publish a book. She took a leap of faith in asking me to write this and not once did she assume I wouldn't be able to. I didn't know I could, but she did and fought for others to believe it too. And without Kate's kindness and loving support, you wouldn't be reading this book either. At times she gently prompted the words out of me and at other times she organised a whole lot of information into order. So much of this book was only an inner knowing and I never had to explain it in words before, but she kept me calm and encouraged the whole way through. I believe women supporting women is necessary if we're going to turn the future of this planet around. This book is full of that and it feels wonderful!

A final special thank you to all at the College of Sound Healing in England for welcoming the strange tapping lady with open arms and helping her work it all out. 'You are a blossoming flower.'

About the Author

Emma WhispersRed first discovered ASMR after a car accident left her with PTSD. She started to create her own videos on YouTube and is now one of the world's most popular ASMRtists. A leading figure within the ASMR community she regularly appears in the media and has worked with brands such as Fuze Tea and Spotify. Emma is a qualified sound therapy practitioner and Reiki healer and lives in London with her family.

▶ WhispersRed ASMR
◎ @WhispersRed_ASMR
f 𝕏 @WhispersRedASMR

Available to download in audiobook formats now

If you enjoyed this book, why not try these three unique audio experiences, created to fit into your busy life:

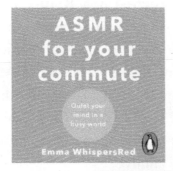
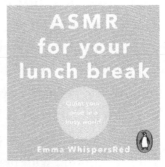

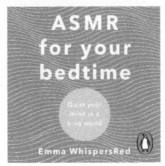

These short audiobooks are perfect for ASMR fans, beginners and those searching for deep, joyful and meditative ways to relax.

Created by Emma WhispersRed

www.penguin.co.uk/unwindyourmind